$7luS$

BI 0111677 0

Birmingham City University
LIBRARY

CITY OF BIRMINGHAM
POLYTECHNIC LIBRARY

AUTHOR   SUPER, D E

TITLE   Occupational psychology

SUBJECT No.   I58.7 | Sup

BOOK No.   01116770

P43036 B1(C)

KV-435-648

BIRMINGHAM CITY
UNIVERSITY
DISCARDED

Occupational Psychology

Behavioral Science in Industry Series

Edited by Victor H. Vroom
Carnegie-Mellon University

MAN-MACHINE ENGINEERING
Alphonse Chapanis, The Johns Hopkins University

OCCUPATIONAL PSYCHOLOGY
Donald E. Super and Martin J. Bohn, Jr.,
Teachers College, Columbia University

ORGANIZATIONAL ANALYSIS:
A SOCIOLOGICAL VIEW
Charles Perrow, The University of Wisconsin

PERSONNEL SELECTION AND PLACEMENT
Marvin D. Dunnette, University of Minnesota

PSYCHOLOGY OF
UNION-MANAGEMENT RELATIONS
Ross Stagner and Hjalmar Rosen,
Wayne State University

SOCIAL PSYCHOLOGY OF
THE WORK ORGANIZATION
Arnold S. Tannenbaum, The University of Michigan

TRAINING IN INDUSTRY:
THE MANAGEMENT OF LEARNING
Bernard M. Bass and James A. Vaughan,
The University of Rochester

CONSUMER BEHAVIOR:
A PSYCHOLOGICAL INTERPRETATION
Robert Perloff, Purdue University

Occupational
Psychology

Donald E. Super
Martin J. Bohn, Jr.
Teachers College
Columbia University

CITY OF BIRMINGHAM LIBRARY POLYTECHNIC

Tavistock Publications

... HAM ... LIBRARY

BOOK No. 01116770

S. N. 158·7/Sup

First published in Great Britain in 1971
by Tavistock Publications Limited
11 New Fetter Lane, London EC4.
Printed in Great Britain by photolithography
by Latimer Trend & Co. Ltd.

SBN 422 98600 3

© 1970 by Wadsworth Publishing Company, Inc. Belmont,
California 94002. All rights reserved. No part of this
book may be reproduced, stored in a retrieval system or
transcribed, in any form or by any means, electronic,
mechanical, photocopying, recording, or otherwise, without
the prior written permission of the publisher.

foreword

The heterogeneity of behavioral science in industry makes it impossible for a single author to do justice to the subject's many facets in a single text. Although full-length volumes on particular topics are available for the specialist, these books are often beyond the level of the advanced undergraduate or beginning graduate student, and they typically go into more detail than is justified in a general course. To meet the changing educational needs generated by this complex subject matter, the Behavioral Science in Industry series was conceived.

The concept is simple. Leading authorities have written short books, at a fairly basic level, to present the essentials of particular fields of inquiry. These books are designed to be used in combination, as a basic text for courses in industrial psychology or behavioral science in industry, or singly, as supplementary texts or collateral reading in more specialized courses.

To implement this concept, the editor outlined the general scope of the series, specified a list of titles, and sketched the content of each volume. Leading social scientists nominated authors for each of the proposed books, and, in following up these leads, the editor was extremely fortunate in enlisting the enthusiastic cooperation of the kinds of men who are not only specialists in their subjects, but who can communicate their ideas in highly readable fashion.

The need for such a series is apparent from the marked changes that have occurred in the last two or three decades in the application of the scientific method to the study of human behavior at work. Perhaps the most significant of these changes is the extension of the range of problems subjected to systematic research. The continuing concern of industrial psychology with methods of assessing individual differences for the selection and placement of personnel has been supplemented by intensive research on such diverse topics as leadership and supervision, the design of man-machine systems, consumer preferences, management development, career patterns, and union-management relations.

This expanding focus of industrial psychology has been accompanied by changes in the objectives and strategies of research. Research has become less concerned with techniques for solving particular problems and more concerned with shedding light on the processes that underlie various behavioral phenomena, on the assumption that improvements in technology will be facilitated by a better understanding of these processes. To implement these new objectives, the psychometric and correlational methods of research in personnel selection and placement were adapted to new problems and supplemented by experiments in laboratory and field settings. As a result, the study of behavior in industrial organizations has been undertaken by researchers who have not previously been identified with industrial psychology. Experimental psychologists investigated problems of human factors in equipment design; social psychologists worked on problems of leadership, communication, and social influence; and clinical psychologists applied their diagnostic and therapeutic skills in industrial settings.

The net effect has been a blurring of the boundary lines among these subdisciplines and a growing recognition of the interdependence of "basic" and "applied" research. These changes have also obscured lines of demarcation among disciplines and professions. Psychologists, sociologists, cultural anthropologists, political scientists, and economists, and specialists in such functional managerial fields as production, labor relations, marketing, and accounting have discovered that much of their work is interrelated and that their interests are often mutual. The resultant cross-fertilization has given an interdisciplinary character to much of the new research and has afforded some currency to the interdisciplinary label *behavioral science*.

This series has been planned to reflect these changes in subject matter and research methods and to provide the reader with a valuable summary of the current status of behavioral science in industry.

Victor H. Vroom

preface

The purpose of this book is to bring together in a readable way what psychologists have learned about occupations and careers. The focus is on what we know. The objective is to make this knowledge available in a way that is clear, interesting, and meaningful to readers who may have little or no background in psychology. The way chosen to present the information should make it helpful also to those who have had previous work in differential, developmental, or other fields of psychology that are basic to occupational psychology and to those who are interested in applications, especially in applications to work and to careers, of psychology.

Some attention is paid to how we know what we know, so that the skeptical or inquiring reader may develop some understanding of the methods of psychology, of that which makes it a science rather than an art or a collection of folklore. But methodology is subordinated to problems, to principles, and to solutions.

We have had in mind audiences of undergraduates and of inquiring adults. In writing for these groups, we believe we have also written for beginning graduate students in need of a synthesis, for business and industrial executives who want an overview, for school counselors, for social workers and psychiatrists who seek better to understand the psychology of work and of careers, and for those who in mid-career are moved to take stock of themselves and of their situations and look to psychology for help.

The book begins with a discussion of the relevance of occupational psychology, of what it is and why it is important. It then takes up individual differences in abilities, interests, values, and personality, and brings together what we know about the role that these play in occupational choice and adjustment. The concept of careers is then examined, and the importance of a *developmental* approach to occupational psychology, as well as of the more traditional *differential* approach, is made clear. The concern is not only with knowledge leading to the matching of men and jobs, but with understanding that helps in guiding human development, in facilitating self-actualization in ways that benefit both the individual and society. Finally, the focus shifts to applications in personnel work and in vocational counseling and to the use of occupational psychology in industrial and educational institutions.

The helpful suggestions of the reviewers, Dr. Anne Roe and Dr. Victor Vroom, are gratefully acknowledged. The junior author's wife, Dr. Suzanne Erbe Bohn, made many helpful suggestions for improved coverage and clarity, while the senior author's wife, veteran of many manuscripts and several prefaces, took this one in her stride.

Donald E. Super
Martin J. Bohn, Jr.

contents

chapter one

What Is Occupational Psychology?

What is occupational psychology, and why learn something about it? Is it relevant to modern needs? Does it have any validity?

It is as relevant as finding and playing an appropriate role in society, as having an identity of one's own, as doing one's thing, as having a means of self-support, as getting and holding a job, or as eventually retiring.

It is as valid as people are willing to be, as real as the sweat on one's brow, as meaningful as the feeling of mastery that comes with a difficult task well done, as worthwhile as the object made or as the service rendered.

Occupational psychology has traditionally been *differential psychology* applied to occupations—to occupational choice, selection, success, and satisfaction. Occupational psychology has become *developmental psychology* applied to vocations, to the processes of developing vocational preferences, choosing an occupation, entering it, succeeding, obtaining satisfaction in it, and moving from one position to another as the career unfolds. Like other applied sciences, occupational psychology today is different in fundamental ways than it was a generation or two ago.

Two generations ago, early in the twentieth century, individual differences were for the first time being scientifically studied, and their relevance to work, to occupational choice and success, was not yet known.

One generation ago, by the 1930s, midway between the two world wars, a number of different kinds of aptitudes, interests, values, needs, and personality traits had been identified and measured. Their role in occupational success and satisfaction had become fairly clear; vocational guidance and personnel selection on bases other than education, work experience, family, or personal impressions became possible. To use an oversimplified explanation, square pegs were to be guided into square holes, and square holes were to be filled with square pegs.

Today we know that both holes and pegs change shape, and that any one peg occupies more than one hole during the course of a lifetime. Individual differences are still important. Their relationships to occupations and to success are still studied and put to use, but human development and change are also taken into account. The stages of development that people undergo, the problems of choice and adjustment that they encounter at different periods in their lives, and the methods that they use in coping with adjustment tasks are now known to be important. So are the aptitudes and interests that affect people's choices and that enable them to apply themselves with varying degrees of success and satisfaction to the tasks of the moment or of the life stage. Situational determinants are also taken into account, as society's expectations of the individual change with his increasing maturity, and as society's needs for certain skills are studied by occupational sociologists and by manpower economists.

Work, paid employment, may some day cease to be relevant and valid for most people because automation could conceivably produce all of the goods and most of the services that man needs. But occupations, in the fundamental sense of that word, will always be relevant and, it is hoped, valid, for man will need to occupy his time, to use his skills, and to find outlets for his interests. The successive and concurrent occupations of any one man may be more varied than they are today, for they may be avocational. A man may not need to earn a livelihood by means of them, since the automated economy may provide his livelihood. But occupied he will be, in a sound society, for his own mental health and for society's well-being. And careers will be pursued, for even without an occupation a man's life will unfold willy-nilly. A life that has some structure, some sequence, some order imposed by the abilities and interests of the individual interacting with the conditions and demands of society is likely to be more satisfying than a life that lacks structure and that is not guided by the inner capacities of the man or woman living it.

The specific substance of occupational psychology will therefore change with the generations, as the economy changes. But its psychological determinants will remain the same, as long as men have verbal esthetic values. And the life-stage structure will remain the same, as long as men are born young, develop and mature, and grow old.

This is why the study of occupational psychology, of individual differences and career patterns, will remain relevant and valid.

Part One of this book deals with individual differences and with some problems of their measurement. Part Two considers them as the psychological basis for the division of labor, taking up occupational ability and personality patterns. Part Three then deals with career development, shifting the focus from the traditional matching of men and jobs to a current dynamic view of man developing, choosing, and adapting. Finally, Part Four points up applications to personnel selection and development and to vocational guidance and counseling.

part one

Individual Differences

The eighteenth century discovered man, the nineteenth century sought to set him free, and the twentieth century is now concerned with helping him to achieve self-fulfillment. The philosophers and political scientists of the Age of Enlightenment wrote and talked about the rights of man, seeking to clarify the origins and nature of these rights and considering the type of government needed to ensure them. These men paved the way for the revolutions which, late in the eighteenth century, began the work of creating such governments. The reformers of the nineteenth century began to rebuild society along new lines. They broadened the franchise by giving the vote to the common man and by educating him so that he could use it wisely. They emancipated the slaves, and they made it possible for individuals to join in collective bargaining in order to strengthen their voices. The twentieth century has carried on these movements. It has studied man in order to understand better his nature, his needs, and his potential and to find ways of helping him to realize his potential.

Sir Francis Galton, it is true, had begun the study of individual differences in England almost a generation after the first major electoral reforms and the abolition of slavery in his country. In America, J. McKeen Cattell had attempted to measure intelligence before the end of the same century, also about a generation after emancipation in his own country. But it was not until after the turn of the century that the study of individual differences in intelligence took practical form and the implications of these differences for education, for vocational counseling, and for personnel selection began to be clear.

With the development and improvement of instruments, systematic study of individual differences became possible. Attention could be paid to social and ethical questions raised by the use of tests. We now ask not only "How able does the test show the candidate to be?" but also "How able was the candidate to show his ability on the test used?" and "How legitimate is it to make such an assessment in this case with this instrument?"

In Part I, Chapter 2 deals with the ways in which people differ psychologically, with the problems of actual and potential abilities, and with the ways in which individual differences are reflected in occupations. The nature and development of the various kinds of aptitudes and motivations (interests, values, needs, etc.) are considered. Their predictive validity for occupations and assessment is touched upon.

In the process of surveying, in Chapter 2, the ways in which people differ psychologically, we shall also briefly consider the methods of measuring these psychological characteristics, for the nature of the aptitude or trait is in part defined by the method by which it is judged. Chapter 3 will consider more explicitly some problems of measurement and assessment that also are necessary to an understanding of human differences. Chapters 4 and 5 will deal in more detail with the psychological bases of the division of labor as revealed in occupational ability and personality patterns. Chapters 6 and 7 will shift focus from differential to developmental psychology, dealing with vocational or career development.

It has frequently been pointed out that the psychology of individual differences is the cornerstone of occupational psychology. Part I therefore deals with that cornerstone as a basis for subsequent consideration of the psychological division of labor, of the determinants of career development, and of vocational guidance and personnel selection.

chapter two

How People Differ

All men are created equal—but no two men are alike. Is there, in these two widely accepted sayings, a contradiction that lies at the root of many of our current social difficulties and disturbances? Or is there only an apparent contradiction, arising from differing interpretations of these aphorisms? An enduring problem of understanding is suggested by the familiar formulation to the effect that "All men are equal, but some men are more equal than others."

Equality and Difference

Equality could, in this context, mean equality in value, in human qualities, in essential and potential goodness regardless of ability, prestige, or power. This is the meaning that is revealed by the Declaration of the Rights of Man, the preamble to the Constitution of the United States, and other famous documents of the eighteenth-century enlightenment and revolutions. Equality could also mean equal in ability and in readiness to contribute to society, and this interpretation is indeed sometimes made.

Actuality and Potentiality

Confusing the choice of meanings is the difference between actuality and potentiality. One may assume that the essential human worth of all men and man's right to develop his potentialities to their fullest are valid concepts. There is still the question of differences in actual ability and in capacity or potential for development. Actual dif-

8

ferences in ability seem clear enough: some people do run faster, solve more complex mathematical problems, write better books, or sing better than others do. Differences in potential, though, cause confusion and even disagreement among experts. The best evidence available a generation ago was interpreted as showing that intelligence is largely inherited and that hereditary differences are considerable. But the best evidence now available is interpreted by most psychologists and other behavioral scientists as showing that, although great individual differences in human characteristics do exist, they are much more the product of experience and much more modifiable than was once believed. That many people, because of cultural disadvantages, do less well on aptitude tests than they otherwise might seems fairly well established. The elimination of educational and social disadvantages would therefore change the position of some persons on the scale of ability. But that there are great differences in abilities even in educationally and socially privileged groups is sometimes lost from sight in the fervor of social justice. It therefore seems to many behavioral scientists that individual differences are here to stay, although they would be more equitably distributed among cultural groups in an affluent and unbiased society.

We may therefore conclude that all men are created equal in essential worth, but that they differ greatly in their human characteristics, both as a result of differences in potential and as a result of experiences affecting the development of that potential.

Individual Differences and Occupations

What have these individual differences to do with occupational psychology, the subject of this book? Occupation being a type of human endeavor, it follows logically that differences in people will be reflected by differences in occupational pursuits and achievements. To cite one more aphorism, if birds of a feather flock together, the men found in one occupation should have some common characteristics that differentiate them from men in other occupations. This tendency, we shall see, is one of the fundamentals of occupational psychology.

Whether these differences between persons engaging in various occupations are the *cause* of entry into the respective occupations or the *result* of engaging in them is an important question. The answer affects policies and practices in education, guidance, training, selection, and induction. If individual differences exist before the sorting of people into occupations takes place, they may be important determinants of success and satisfaction; making use of them in vocational guidance and in personnel selection would be possible and desirable. But if these differences do not exist in any significant degree before occupational training and experience, or if they are produced to any substantial degree by such experience, then to attach importance to them in vocational guidance or selection may be to deprive individuals of opportunities from which they might benefit and occupations in which they might be as successful as others. It would also deprive occupations and enterprises of potentially valuable manpower.

The process of taking on the characteristics or adopting the behaviors of others is known as *socialization*. In the behavioral sciences, the term is applied to the bringing up of children and to the assimilation of people into socioeconomic and occupational groups of which they have not previously been a part. It includes the learning of new attitudes, values, skills, and modes of behavior. Thus, the "self-made man" learns new ways of living, dressing, entertaining, and relaxing as a result of the change in social status accompanying the accumulation of wealth. Thus, also, the child learns table manners, dressing and undressing, the sharing of toys, and sitting still in class, and the adolescent learns to work, to groom himself, to date, and to dance.

Studies of social mobility have shown that a significant part of the socialization process actually takes place prior to the change of status. Similarly, research in child and adolescent development shows that many of the traits and behaviors of older age levels are exhibited to some degree before the individual actually enters the next life stage. The term *anticipatory socialization* refers to the early appearance of differential characteristics in those who later change status: the working-class youth who moves to the middle class tends, in "anticipation," to exhibit middle-class values and behavior before he actually becomes a member of the middle class.

In occupational psychology, the term has not often been used, but the same phenomenon appears to exist. Aptitude and interest profiles of early adolescent boys show the same kinds of differences as those noted in men, although the interest profiles are generally somewhat less well developed. Boys who have a specific occupational goal or who choose a specific field of study in high school and college tend to be differentiated from boys with other objectives, and those who change objectives tend to change to goals that could be predicted by use of their aptitude and interest patterns. The self-concepts of men and women who change occupations are as much like their concepts of the occupation to which they change after a year of full-time training as they are at the beginning of training. The interests of men in an occupation do not change appreciably as a result of long experience in that occupation. The perceptual speed and accuracy of adults who have never been trained or employed as office clerks are unaffected by five months of training, although these aptitudes have been shown to differentiate clerical workers from persons in other occupations and to be correlated with success in clerical work.

There is thus a good deal of evidence that individual differences in intelligence, special aptitudes, interests, and self-concepts exist prior to occupational training and experience and that they are not much affected by later experience in the occupation. It would seem that the characteristics in question were either inborn or the result of pre-occupational experience—of socialization in the family, in the school, or in the neighborhood. But it is difficult to conceive of some of these characteristics as innate: interest in scientific work or the concept of oneself as a psychologist could hardly be inborn, although the capacity to develop such interest or such a self-concept might be. It therefore seems likely that it is prior experience of a relevant type—anticipatory socialization —that develops the potential for the individual differences leading to the choice of a given field of work.

Aptitudes

Some people learn easily and quickly, apparently without strain or effort. For others, learning requires an effort revealed by frowning, hesitation, or mumbling. The former individuals master ideas and skills that are complex and abstract, while the latter are limited in their learning to the simple and the concrete. Individual differences in ability to learn exist in varying degrees and are normally distributed. The term "aptitude," in psychology, is used to denote the capacity for learning.

Direct or Indirect Measurement

It is not possible to measure capacity to learn in the direct manner in which certain other kinds of measurements are made. A man's height, for example, is measured by comparing his actual height with that of another object, such as a yardstick, which serves as a standard measure. But the capacity to learn cannot be directly measured; instead, it can be judged only by what a man does. Measures of learning capacity are therefore contaminated by experience, what one does learn being the result of a combination of capacity to learn and practice in doing what one has already learned.

Let us consider, for example, a standard test of intelligence. One such test, designed for use in the United States, includes a question concerning the name of the first American president. The reasoning behind this question, designed to differentiate at the lower levels of mental ability, is that those who have a certain amount of intellectual capacity will have learned this fact by a certain age and that those who have not learned this familiar fact are low in ability to learn. This reasoning is sound when the test is used with children and adults who have been exposed, while growing up, to typical American experiences. But if the test is used, as it has occasionally been, with displaced persons of German upbringing, with coal miners from Polish Silesia, or with Yemenite Jews—all people who have not been exposed to American history and folklore—knowledge of the name of the first American president is not an accurate measure of ability to learn.

One might say that in physics, too, measurement is achieved only indirectly, by ascertaining what one object or quality does to another. Temperature, for example, is measured by what it does to mercury or alcohol. But the capacity of temperature to alter metal or liquid is not affected by experience: one degree of cold makes the mercury shrink the same amount, no matter how many months of winter have elapsed, no matter how many times the mercury has been exposed to temperature changes. In contrast, how much the child has been exposed to games, books, and tests does, we now know, have important effects on his responses to tests of ability to learn.

An aptitude is, then, a capacity to learn. Learning may deal with different kinds of materials, processes, and concepts, including words, numbers, and other types of symbols such as geometric forms, shapes and sizes, and muscular and skeletal movements.

A moot question among psychologists for many years was whether the nature of aptitudes is unitary or complex: is the same fundamental capacity to learn involved in all of these aptitudes, or are they discrete and independent abilities?

Aptitudes: One or Several?

It was Carl Spearman, an English psychologist, who in the years following World War I led in the development of the theory of one basic aptitude. He called the aptitude "g," for *general factor* or general intelligence. He based his thinking on the finding of one factor underlying all of the tests that he and his students studied by means of factor analysis (a statistical method designed for isolating *one* general factor when such indeed exists). Other *specific factors* were found, too, but each of them appeared only in a single test, and hence was so specific as to be of no apparent scientific or practical interest. Because of the cumbersomeness of factor-analytic methods at that time—before the invention of electronic computers—the number of tests in an experimental battery and the number of subjects taking the tests were severely limited. We shall see that these limitations had important effects on Spearman's findings.

Not long after Spearman's work became known, an American, Louis L. Thurstone, also undertook the factor analysis of batteries of intelligence tests and other presumed aptitude tests. His tests were more numerous and more varied than Spearman's. His factorial methods were designed to maximize the importance of specific factors, rather than to minimize them as had Spearman's. The result was that Thurstone found a number of group factors, reflected in several kinds of tests, as well as specific factors like Spearman's. He therefore developed a *group factor* theory, a theory of several distinct and important aptitudes.

The conflict of methods and views that resulted from the two men's work was resolved, in due course, by improvements in test construction, in factor-analytic and data-processing methods, and in the design of studies. The evidence now points to the existence of 1) a general but not universal factor best called reasoning ability, 2) less general but widespread reasoning or cognitive abilities associated with the type of symbol used and therefore, presumably, with experience, and 3) other less general factors that appear to reflect sensory or motor capacities.

REASONING

The basic capacity for reasoning is what psychologists generally mean when they write or speak of general intelligence. It is, after all, by reasoning about their experiences and observations that men learn, more than by the simple conditioning that characterizes animals in the classical laboratory experiments. The reasoning may be of the sudden, insightful, "aha" type studied by some Gestalt psychologists, or it may be of the more laborious problem-solving (data-collecting, data-analyzing, conclusion-drawing, and conclusion-testing) type analyzed by others with a behavioristic orientation. Intelligence has often been defined as the capacity to solve problems.

Verbal reasoning has been found to be the most universally important kind of reasoning, and verbal intelligence tests the most generally valid intelligence tests. Words being the most important and widely used type of symbol, this is hardly surprising. Mathematics books explain numerical and spatial symbols with words, physical processes are described in words, and, despite the communicative value of facial expressions and gestures, people trying to communicate with a person whose language they do not know often make use of words uttered with increasing volume and rising pitch as they seek to make themselves clear. Analogies often make good reasoning items—for example: *day is to night as white is to*———(the missing word, "black," may be one of five alternatives supplied by the test).

Numerical reasoning is a second variety of reasoning ability; it manifests itself through the manipulation of numerical symbols. The ability to see the type of progression in a series of numbers, whether arithmetic or geometric, is one example of such reasoning. Consider the following problem: Supply the missing number in the series 3,9,27,—. The person answering a question of this type may do it laboriously by verbalizing, or—without the use of words—simply by mentally manipulating the numbers. Our culture being more verbal than numerical, most people are more used to the manipulation of verbal symbols, and persons taking numerical-reasoning tests feel negatively toward the tests they take more often than do those taking verbal-reasoning tests.

Abstract reasoning is a third type of reasoning ability, in which the symbols used are neither verbal nor numerical but abstract—that is, geometric in form. The letters that form words are themselves nothing but symbols to which meaning has been assigned. Numbers are also merely symbols, and similar meanings can be assigned to geometric forms such as triangles, circles, and squares. In fact, some Asian languages such as Singhalese use a kind of script which, to European eyes, is geometric. Abstract-reasoning tests therefore seem the least meaningful type of test to the average subject, but are thought by some psychologists to be most likely to measure pure reasoning ability. An example: □ is to ○ as ▽ is to which of the following: ○○ 0 ⊘ 0 ?

Cultural influences might be expected to have the greatest effect on verbal tests, next greatest effect on numerical tests, and least effect on abstract-reasoning tests, because of the emphasis of both informal and formal education in developing verbal and arithmetic skills. It has been found, however, that familiarity with even the geometric figures used in abstract-reasoning tests is a result of cultural experience: pegboards, building blocks, and puzzles are familiar to children in certain cultures and at certain socioeconomic levels within a given culture, but unknown to others.

The predictive validity of these tests is also, as we shall see in a later chapter, a function of their saturation with the culture. Verbal tools are important in education, in vocational training, and in work. Therefore, the tests that have the closest relation to the criteria of success in this culture are those that assess the extent to which capacity and experience have equipped a person with verbal skills. Tests that are least saturated with the culture (the abstract-reasoning tests) are least effective in predicting what a person will do or how well he will do it because they show least well what he has done with his reasoning abilities in the past.

Reasoning tests, which are widely used as measures of general intelligence, usually contain items of the three types so far discussed, although a few use only one or two types of items. Older tests—for example, the Otis Tests of Mental Ability—tended to mix item content. These are known as "spiral omnibus tests" because they use verbal, numerical, and geometric items arranged in sequence, not according to content, but according to difficulty. More recent tests arrange items by content in separately scorable parts, giving both a total score and part scores for the different types of reasoning ability. This group includes the Wesman Personnel Classification Test, which uses only verbal and arithmetic items, and the Differential Aptitude Tests, whose Verbal, Numerical, and Abstract Reasoning Tests can be combined to yield a general intelligence score. Illustrative of the special or one-type item tests is the Miller Analogies Test, which uses only verbal analogies as means of measuring the academic promise of candidates for graduate study.

SPATIAL VISUALIZATION

The ability to judge shapes and sizes, to visualize the relationships of objects to each other, and to orient oneself in relation to objects is known as spatial visualization or spatial judgment. It is sometimes confused with abstract reasoning, because tests of both types of aptitude often use geometric figures. Visualization tests can be so set up as to permit abstract reasoning to play an important part in the answering process. Some nonverbal mental ability tests, such as the Army Beta of

World War I and its many derivatives, were so constructed. But in groups which are relatively homogeneous intellectually, much lower correlations are found between well devised spatial-visualization tests and reasoning tests than among the various types of reasoning tests themselves.

The work of Spearman and his students led to the identification of spatial-visualization ability, called *k* or practical intelligence in England. In America its identification by Thurstone led to its being called spatial visualization. Figure 2–1 shows a typical item testing this ability, an easy sample question in the Revised Minnesota Paper Form Board.

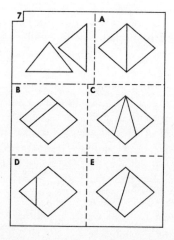

Look at Problem 7. There are two parts in the upper left-hand corner. Now look at the five figures labelled A, B, C, D, E. You are to decide which figure shows how these parts can fit together.

FIGURE 2–1. *Sample question from the Revised Minnesota Paper Form Board. Reproduced by permission. Copyright 1941 by The Psychological Corporation, New York, N.Y. Renewed 1969. All rights reserved.*

PERCEPTUAL SPEED AND ACCURACY

The ability to distinguish one symbol or set of symbols from another soon emerged, in the aptitude research after World War I, as a factor distinct from spatial visualization or the reasoning abilities. Unrelated to either intelligence or spatial judgment, it is the ability to recognize, quickly and accurately, minor differences in words or numbers. The Minnesota Clerical Test (so called because this aptitude is important in many record-keeping activities) has been the most widely used test of this type for more than 30 years. It consists of two parts. One contains pairs of names; some pairs are identical and others different. The other has pairs of numbers, of which some are identical and others different. Typical items follow:

Smith and Co._____Smith and Co.
Johnson and Morris_____Johnston and Morris
James C. Brown_____James C. Brown
19367_____19367
79842_____78942
93784_____93784

The task is, of course, to identify which pairs are alike.

Cultural differences in the less general aptitudes, such as spatial visualization and perceptual speed and accuracy, have been studied less than have those in the more general aptitudes that are known as intelligence. That knowing how to read the Latin alphabet and the European version of Arabic numerals is a help in recognizing similarities and differences in lists using those symbols seems hardly to require proof. Being able to make spatial judgments with geometric figures also requires exposure to the culture of geometry if not to geometry itself. The necessity for such exposure has been shown by attempts to use spatial items in primitive societies and by the inability of children in Western societies who have not had experience with building blocks and construction toys to see meaning in such test items. Experiments have been conducted on the effects of further spatial experience on the aptitudes of American high school graduates. Results show that these aptitudes are not influenced by relevant experience (for example, a one-year course in physics or training in clerical work) beyond that common to most high school students (see Super and Crites [95], Ch. 8 and 11, for a more detailed discussion).

Predictive validity, as we shall see in the discussion of occupational differences, is shown by the fact that the differences in aptitude found between subjects with and subjects without relevant experience are related to the speed and efficiency of learning relevant skills, procedures, and subject matter.

MANUAL DEXTERITIES

The aptitudes discussed so far are largely mental, whether intellectual in the strict sense of this term or perceptual. There is, however, a constellation of aptitudes that are strictly motor—those normally referred to as manual dexterity. Despite the frequent use of the singular noun, these aptitudes are actually plural; even the term "constellation" is something of a misnomer. Fine manual or finger dexterity (often measured by the speed with which small pins can be put in holes or by the number of nuts and bolts assembled in a given amount of time) has been proved to be independent of gross manual or arm-and-hand dexterity (measured by ability to reach for and grasp disks an inch or two in diameter and an inch thick and place them in evenly spaced holes in a large board). Figures 2–2 and 2–3 show, respectively, the Crawford Small Parts Test and the Stromberg Dexterity Test as typical examples.

FIGURE 2–2. *Crawford Small Parts Test. Courtesy of The Psychological Corporation, 304 East 45th Street, New York, N.Y. 10017.*

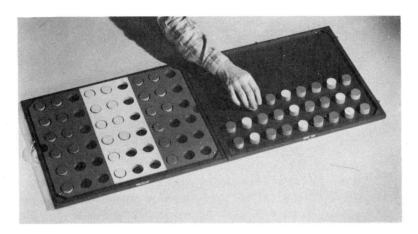

FIGURE 2-3. *Stromberg Dexterity Test. Courtesy of The Psychological Corporation, 304 East 45th Street, New York, N.Y. 10017.*

A frequent source of confusion has been that such tests measure quite different and independent kinds of manual dexterity rather than general dexterity. The nature of manual aptitudes is another problem. Aptitude means capacity to learn as shown by how well one has learned to use a basic skill; for example, how many words one *has* learned is indicative of how fast one *will* learn history or algebra. What, one must then ask, does the speed with which one has learned to manipulate small blocks or nuts and bolts indicate about future learning? Logically, the results of a manual-aptitude test should give some indication of how quickly the subject will master a new manual task or how difficult a manual skill he will be able to acquire. We shall see, when dealing with occupational implications, that manual-dexterity tests are aptitude tests in the sense that they indicate something about future learning. We shall also see that both perceptual and motor skills are related, in some situations, not only to learning but also to productivity—in other words, that tests of manual dexterity sometimes measure proficiency as well as aptitude.

Simple vs. Complex Aptitudes

The aptitudes discussed so far, it should be noted, have all been described in psychological terms and have been found to be relatively discrete and unitary characteristics. Factor analysis is, after all, a method of breaking the complex down into the simple or basic. But there is a long-established popular tendency, reflected also in vocational psychology, to think in terms of occupations and occupational aptitudes; thus we refer to mechanical aptitude, musical aptitude, artistic ability, and medical aptitude. In one sense this usage is correct: people do differ in their capacity to become good auto mechanics, to play the piano, to master water-color painting, and to learn medicine. In another sense this usage is quite wrong: there is no such entity as aptitude for medicine, no one psychological characteristic of which a substantial amount is essential for success in music or art or mechanics.

Aptitude for medicine, so far as we now know, is a combination of verbal reasoning ability, scientific interest, experience with the biological sciences, and status drive. The only aptitude known to be involved is verbal reasoning.

Artistic aptitude is also a complex of general and specific aptitudes, interest, and motivation. Esthetic judgment, most commonly measured by the Meier Art Judgment Test, is often referred to as artistic ability, but it may prove to be a combination of spatial visualization (with which it is correlated) and artistic experience (not formal training but exposure to good art forms).

Musical aptitude is another complex of rather narrowly definable capacities and motivational variables. The ability to make fine discriminations of pitch or rhythm is not unitary, for each of the musical capacities is relatively distinct. Most of the study of musical aptitude was done on the musical-aptitude tests most widely used before the development of refined statistical methods, and little progress has been made since then in studying aptitude for music. It does seem clear that there is a complex rather than one musical aptitude, but what constitutes the complex is not clear.

Mechanical aptitude has been more continuously, more thoroughly, and more successfully studied. What we usually call by this name has been found to be a complex—perhaps one should say a hodgepodge—of other aptitudes and characteristics. It consists, in degrees that vary with the test, of spatial visualization, mechanical information or experience, and reasoning (verbal, numerical, and abstract). Despite its complexity, it functions fairly well when treated as a unitary aptitude, for it has been shown to predict the speed and facility with which people learn mechanical and scientific principles and master relevant skills. It differentiates men who enter and remain in mechanical and technical occupations from men who enter other fields of work.

Motivation

Some people could learn if they would make the effort but do not make the effort. Aptitudes therefore are unused or only partly used, and the individual's achievement is not equal to his promise. We have all said, "I could have done better, but I wasn't that interested," in connection with a course of study, a tennis match, a sales campaign, or a committee's preparation for some big event. When falling back on the motivational explanation one may be rationalizing, giving a socially acceptable excuse whether or not it is true, or one may be stating an actual fact. In either case, the role commonly attributed to individual differences in motivation is made clear.

Motivation has long been a subject of study in the psychological laboratory, especially with animal subjects, whose physical condition and environment are more readily controlled and manipulated than are those of human beings. It has also long been studied by social psychologists, personality theorists, sales and consumer psychologists, and vocational psychologists, often with differing definitions and methods. Of all of these, two definitions have had clear implications for occupational psychology, and the related instruments and resulting studies have led to findings that are relevant to the understanding of individual differences in occupational behavior. These definitions or aspects of motivation are *needs* and *interests*. Also to be considered are *personality traits, adjustment,* and *values.*

Needs

Need is defined as a lack of something which, if it were present, would contribute to the well-being of the organism. It is a condition that is lacking, a force that organizes behavior, driving the individual to act (or not to act) in certain ways in order to change an unsatisfying condition. The tension created by such a lack is sometimes called a *drive,* but is also sometimes comprehended under the term *need.* While the distinction between drive and need may seem logical, it has in practice not generally been made. For example, Murray's Thematic Apperception Test and the Edwards Personal Preference Schedule, both developed and widely used to measure the strength of needs in the individual, do not attempt to separate the lack from the drive to reduce the resulting tension. In Murray's terminology, thirst—the need for water—and need achievement—the drive to do one's best—combine in a meaningful way the concept of a lack and that of a drive to do something about it. In some respects, need is the most basic of personality constructs, since it can be used to explain even the most elementary, physiologically based behavior.

The categorization of needs developed by Maslow (62) has found favor in occupational psychology. In this organization of needs, stressing man's basic goodness and his potential for worthwhile achievement, Maslow included needs from the basic physical necessities to the most advanced level of psychological development and self-actualization. He presents these needs in their order of prepotency; that is, the more basic needs must be met before the person can be aware of and attend to more derivative needs. For example, people tend to make sure that they have food and shelter before they spend significant amounts of time and energy on beauty or understanding. If the basic needs are not at least partly met, the organism does not survive to consider the higher-level needs such as self-esteem or self-actualization.

Maslow's list of needs, in their order of prepotency, are as follows:

1. Physiological needs

2. Safety needs

3. Belongingness and love

4. Importance, respect, self-esteem

5. Information

6. Understanding

7. Beauty

8. Self-actualization

Most of the needs in this list are adequately described by their names, although the needs for information and for understanding are difficult to differentiate and might best be treated as one, and the need for self-actualization has been viewed by some as so important that it may be a fundamental rather than a higher-order or late-appearing need. It has been suggested, for example, that the willingness to risk the sacrifice of oneself for one's fellows or for a cause—in other words, martyrdom—is evidence that self-actualization is more important to some people than safety. The same might be said of respect and self-esteem, for which safety and physiological needs are frequently overlooked by people under pressure. The needs that appear last in Maslow's hierarchy are probably those in the development of which social learning plays the greatest part; they may, therefore, be either little developed or highly developed; and, if highly developed, they become stronger than other needs that have been satisfied in the past and that continue to be readily met.

Anne Roe (74) made considerable use of Maslow's theory in studying personality in occupations. In particular, she took the position that if a need is not allowed any expression in early childhood it will be expunged and cease to exist for that individual. If the need is only partly satisfied, the person's appetite will be whetted, and the need will become a dominant drive in that person's life. Cultural and familial influences are thus considered crucial.

The other major personality formulation centering around needs is that of Henry Murray (66), whose theorizing based on psychoanalytic thinking led not only to the construct of needs characterizing persons but also to the construct of "press," the pressures that are the environmental determinants of behavior. Certain presses are conducive to seeking to meet certain needs. Thus there is pressure from parents to achieve, which evokes the need in the child to achieve. As a person gains more understanding of his own needs and the relevant presses, he can become more discriminating in choosing tension-reducing behaviors. The lists of needs developed by Murray and Maslow bear considerable similarity to each other, as might be expected, but differ in detail. Murray's theory has led to more attempts at measurement, because of his own early work, while Maslow's scheme has recently had more appeal to occupational psychologists.

Murray's scheme, having led to the development of projective, expressive, and inventory measures, has lent itself more readily to research. His long list of needs reflects origins in psychopathology rather than in psychological assets. The operation of the drives that underlie everyday behavior may be different from that of maladjusted behavior. Murray's list, shortened by Edwards for his Personal Preference Schedule, follows:

1. Achievement
2. Deference
3. Order
4. Exhibition
5. Autonomy
6. Affiliation
7. Intraception (Subjectivism)
8. Succorance

9. Dominance   13. Endurance

10. Abasement   14. Heterosexuality

11. Nurturance   15. Aggression

12. Change

Murray developed a story-construction test in order to assess needs as shown in the themes of the stories, a time-consuming and somewhat unreliable method of measurement. Various sentence-completion tests are easier to give and to score. Edwards' inventory was designed to obtain greater reliability and to save time in administration and scoring. That these three types of need measures—story construction, sentence completion, and personal preference—do indeed assess the same needs is not well demonstrated, and it may be that they tap needs at different levels of awareness or that some or all of these instruments are not satisfactory measuring instruments.

The differential and predictive validity of measures that purport to assess needs has been too little studied to permit sound generalizations concerning the relationships between needs and occupations. Some such relationships have been found, and will be discussed in Chapter 5.

Personality Traits and Adjustment

The need to do, to have, or to be something can logically be expected to lead, with experience, to the development of two types of human characteristics: traits and values. *Traits* are modes of behavior or tendencies to act in certain ways. They may be derived from needs, as ways of acting in order to meet a need in a given type of situation. *Adjustment* is a general quality of behavior, a constellation of tendencies or traits. *Values* are objectives that one seeks to attain. They therefore may be considered objectives that are chosen to satisfy a need.

Trait lists are numerous, somewhat overlapping, and often long, for behavior may be classified in innumerable ways. At times trait lists resemble lists of needs, at other points they resemble lists of values, and sometimes they are difficult to differentiate from interests. The distinctions simply are not clear. Thus Murray lists dominance among his needs, while Allport includes it as a trait in a personality inventory. Murray lists a need to nurture or to help, Eduard Spranger includes social or altruistic values in his list of six, and Gordon Allport and Philip Vernon measure social values in their inventory. Trait inventories and checklists have become almost as numerous as the traits themselves, for drawing up a good list of adjectives is not difficult. Demonstrating that the presumed traits differentiate relevant groups of people and predict behavior in various occupations is much more difficult.

There is, despite these problems, some evidence that personality traits have a bearing on occupational behavior, affecting both choice of occupation and success. (Chapter 5 deals with the relationship in more detail.) Salesmen do make somewhat higher dominance scores than bookkeepers. But, despite such differences, there is a great deal of overlapping of occupations on such traits, and successful workers do not differ clearly from less successful. The best general conclusion appears to be that there is room for many different personalities in any one occupation, and that people with a given set of personality traits find outlets for their behavior tendencies and personal styles in many occupations.

Adjustment is another term or construct often used in organizing data and ideas concerning behavior tendencies. Ways of acting—traits —may be viewed as facilitating or handicapping adjustment, and behavior may be classified as adjustive or nonadjustive in its outcomes.

Thus the sentence-completion test devised by Julian Rotter can be scored for total adjustment (a measure of conflict or harmony between the individual and his life situation), while other very similar instruments are scored for needs resembling those assessed by Murray's thematically analyzed story-construction test and Edwards' inventory. The adjective checklist developed by Harrison Gough can be scored for traits, like J. P. Guilford's inventory and the widely used California and Minnesota inventories, for adjustment as shown by self-esteem or self-acceptance, as is done with Robert Bills' inventory, or for needs, according to Murray's scheme.

Adjustment tests and inventories do not differentiate one occupational group from another. As might be expected, no occupation has a monopoly of well-adjusted or of poorly adjusted people, partly because of the complexity of the determinants of occupational choice and partly because of the varieties of adjustment and maladjustment.

Values

Values have already been defined as objectives that are considered desirable and that are sought in action. They are abstractions—for example, social welfare, power, prestige, understanding, variety, way of life, communion with man or God.

Types of values vary with the perspective of the philosopher or psychologist. The philosopher Eduard Spranger developed a theory that postulated six types of values: theoretical, social (altruistic), political (prestige and power), economic (material), esthetic, and religious (mystical). He believed that men could also be classified into these types. His theory was modified by Allport and Vernon (2) when they developed their values inventory. They treated values as continua—that is, as characteristics existing in some degree in most men—rather than as discrete types of an all-or-none quality.

Empirical researchers have asked men what they seek in life or in their work and have developed longer lists of values. Richard Centers thus identified some fifteen values sought in work or occupations, and most studies of job satisfaction have proposed similar lists of what men and women want in a job. The work-values inventory developed by the senior author (94) for use in vocational counseling with high school students and adults is scored for the following typical 15 values:

1. Altruism
2. Esthetics
3. Creativity
4. Intellectual Stimulation
5. Independence
6. Achievement
7. Prestige
8. Management
9. Economic Returns
10. Security
11. Surroundings
12. Supervisory Relations
13. Associates
14. Variety
15. Way of Life

Some of the values sought in work closely resemble those in the philosophically derived and empirically confirmed lists of Spranger and of Allport and Vernon. The first two values are identical with their similarly named constructs. Intellectual stimulation overlaps considerably with the notion of seeking to know and to understand contained in the Allport-Vernon theoretical value, prestige taps the political value assessed by Allport and Vernon, and the value of economic returns is similar to their notion of economic or material value. But a number of the other values in the work-values inventory are more mundane and less philosophical. They have to do with seeking to control one's own behavior (independence), to plan and supervise work (management), to be able to count on having work (security), and to avoid monotony (variety).

Some values are more characteristic of able, educated, economically favored people, whereas others are sought more by less favored people who have not had opportunity to develop the higher-level values. It appears that a degree of security may be necessary before most people can attach much importance to beauty or to creativity. The theory of the prepotency of some needs developed by Maslow and applied by Roe to occupations seems to be relevant also to values, perhaps because values are derived from needs. In any case, the evidence is clear, in Centers' work for example, that white-collar workers attach more importance to values such as intellectual stimulation and esthetics than do blue-collar workers, who themselves value security and variety more.

Cultural influences play a major role in the development of values, as they do in the development of needs and traits. Even over the span of a decade the dominant values of college students change: security and way of life were stressed most in the generation of students that followed World War II (the era of "privatism"), achievement motivation was strong in the Sputnik era and the Cold War, and altruism and independence became more important with the rediscovery of poverty and the reaction against the war in Vietnam. The conditions and events of the time help shape the objectives that seem important to men.

The differential and predictive validity of measures of values has been studied only to a limited degree. Evidence about occupational differences in values is actually quite satisfactory, for, as will be seen in Chapter 5, people in various occupations do have characteristic value patterns: engineers tend to place relatively low value on esthetics, and school counselors are higher on altruism than are machinists. But it is not established that putting more emphasis on certain values than on others is in any way related to success in an occupation, for too few longitudinal studies have been completed with success criteria collected after testing.

Interests

Values are the objectives that people seek; interests are the activities and objects through which they seek them. People who value knowing and understanding (theoretical or intellectual values) tend to be interested in philosophy or science (two words with similar original meanings, Greek for love of knowledge and Latin for knowledge). Those who value economic returns tend to be interested in business management. Those who place great value on esthetics tend to be interested in art, literature, or music. And those who place most emphasis on variety and independence tend to be interested less in what they do than in the conditions under which they do it.

Despite this correspondence of values and interests, the relationships are not as clear and simple as they might appear, because a given value may be achieved by means of more than one activity or object, and any one activity or object may provide the means of attaining more than one value. It has been found, for example, that some freshman engineering students conceive of engineering as an intellectual occupation, while others see it as, in varying degrees, altruistic, materialistic, or prestigious. These ways of seeing no doubt change with experience and understanding and have some bearing on whether or not a person continues to pursue the activity.

Types of interests identified by various researchers have varied with the instruments used and with the persons studied; as always happens with empirical work, findings are limited by the nature of the data with which the work is done. Virtually all of the work in the psychology of interests has been done by American psychologists who have a strongly empirical orientation; theory has been derived from data rather than data collection being based on theoretical formulations.

Three researchers—Edward K. Strong, G. F. Kuder, and J. P. Guilford—have contributed most heavily to knowledge in this area, with current work being carried on particularly by David Campbell and Kenneth Clark. The interests that differentiate men and women in one occupation from those in others were analyzed by Strong, who, working largely with college students and graduates, studied the groups into which they fell. Classifying activities on a priori grounds and refining his categories by statistical methods, Kuder identified fields of interest that were relatively homogeneous and somewhat independent of each other. Guilford built on the work of Strong and Kuder and carried further the factor-analytic work that Strong had begun. The three resulting lists of types of interests are shown below.

Strong's *Occupational Groups*	*Kuder's* *Interest Fields*	*Guilford's* *Interest Factors*
Biological Science	Scientific	Scientific
Physical Science	Mechanical	Mechanical
Technical	Outdoor	Outdoor
Social Welfare	Social Service	Social Welfare
Business Detail	Clerical	Clerical
Business Contact	Computational	Business
Literary and Legal	Persuasive	Esthetic Expression
	Literary	Esthetic Appreciation
	Artistic	
	Musical	

There are obvious similarities in the three lists, despite differences in types of inventory content and in methods of developing scoring keys and norms. There are also some important differences, but these result from such artifacts as the limited number of musical and artistic occupations studied by Strong, the relatively small number of biological-science items used by Kuder, and the number and variety of items used by Guilford.

In later work, Clark (21) pursued the problem of interest measurement in men employed in skilled and, to a lesser extent, in semiskilled occupations. Early work raised the question of whether such men and women are indeed characterized by distinctive interests: just as the term "semiskilled" means relatively undifferentiated by skill, so it might also mean relatively undifferentiated by interests—"semi-interested." Strong refined and tested the relevant hypotheses, and found (before it was fashionable to pay attention to such matters) that if socioeconomic status is taken into account, men in the skilled occupations can be differentiated from each other by means of their interests. Clark carried the approach further, with more appropriate test content and better occupational samples, but he too concentrated on skilled workers and did little with semiskilled and unskilled workers. Our knowledge of individual differences in interests at these two lowest socioeconomic levels is, therefore, still embryonic. But it does seem likely that people who have not been adequately exposed to varied activities and objects would fail to develop the differentiated interests that characterize those who have had such exposure.

Cultural influences, we must therefore conclude, are particularly important in the development of interests. Longitudinal studies of interests in adolescence have shown that, in most people, measured interests (as contrasted with expressed preferences) are rather stable from the early teens on, and are so especially after the early twenties. Although there are occasional cases of dramatic changes in measured interests, it seems that most middle-class Americans have a sufficient variety of experience with different types of activities and materials to enable them to develop rather stable interest patterns by the time they are 14 or 15 years old. The specific activity or occupation preferred may change, but the type tends to remain constant. Thus, for example, an interest in sociology may replace plans to major in history, but the social-science interest persists. One important exception to this generalization is the development of scientific and technical interests in boys, many of whom outgrow these interests in the teens and develop more interest in literary and artistic, social-service, and business activities as they approach or enter the twenties. Unfortunately, it is not clear ahead of time just who will and who will not continue to have scientific and technical interests in adulthood, although there are some clues from intensive case studies.

The predictive validity of interests is clear, as far as occupational choice is concerned, from studies of the relationships of inventory scores in high school and college to major field in college and to adult occupation. Although measured interests predict no more accurately than do expressed preferences in boys and men of the highest socio-economic level (whose preferences are often determined more by family tradition and status than by satisfying experience based on the rewarded use of abilities), they do give a better indication than do expressed preferences of what a middle-class boy will do when he is an adult. (Apparently, in these cases, ability leads to the development of interest, which then guides decisions, rather than decisions being based on the family's vested interests and preconceived preferences.) Just how interests operate in boys and girls from the less advantaged socio-economic levels is not known, as they have not been studied, but presumably what is true of the top of the socioeconomic scale will prove to be true of the bottom: environmental pressures tend to be stronger than personal abilities and the interests that might develop with the use of these abilities.

Interest being one manifestation of motivation, one might hypothesize that it would predict degree of success as well as field of choice: the more highly motivated person would be more likely to try harder and to get better results. This has been found to be the case in a few occupations—life-insurance sales, for example: men who find the work more congenial tend to sell more insurance. But in most fields, whether of study or of work, this has not been the case. It seems that interest determines whether or not one continues in an activity, but that success in it depends more on other factors. Students do well even in courses they do not like if they want good grades for other reasons, and workmen do a job well, regardless of interest, if they want to be paid or if self-respect and peer acceptance require good work.

Achievement

It may seem unnecessary to point out that people differ not only in aptitudes and in motivation, but also in achievement. Observation of others in school, on the athletic fields, in social activities, in their ways of life, and in their occupations is a constant reminder of this difference. Furthermore, this chapter has shown something of the ways in which fundamental differences in aptitudes and in motivation contribute to individual differences in how much and how well people do.

But achievement is not just a consequence, it is also a cause: differences in achievement in the past tend to be related to differences in achievement in the future. It is an accepted conclusion, well supported by many studies of success in school, in college, in civic life, and in work, that what and how well a person will do in the future can be predicted by examination of what and how well he has done in the past. A past can be an asset or a liability. It can be lived up to, barring important situational changes, and it can fortunately be lived down, given the needed motivation and opportunities. The important point is that the past merits being known and taken into account in considering the future.

Summary

This chapter has briefly examined the constructs or ideas of equality and difference, leading to a survey of ways in which people differ psychologically. These differences have been seen to involve (1) aptitudes—that is, how easily people can learn to do certain kinds of things, (2) motivation, or how people differ in their need and desire to be, have, or do certain kinds of things, and (3) achievement, or how people differ in what they actually become, obtain, and do.

These differences have been seen to be affected, in varying degrees, by the experiences to which the individual is exposed, but to exist in significant degrees even when experiences are very similar. They are assessed by a variety of methods, not only in interviews, which are analyzed by standard methods, but also by story-construction tests, inventories, completion tests, and tests that confront the person being examined with problems that he must solve or tasks that he must perform.

Scores made on these various measures of aptitudes and motivations are related to the type and level of educational and vocational activity subsequently engaged in, to success in learning new skills and in mastering new knowledge (in the case of aptitudes), to success in doing certain kinds of work (in the case of motivation), and to satisfaction in work (also in the case of motivation). The best generalization about aptitude and success, however, is that aptitude is more important for mastery of a field and for establishment in that field than for success once one is established. The best generalization for motivation is that it plays a larger role in determining the direction of effort than in the degree of success attained as a result of making the effort. These topics are considered in more detail in subsequent chapters.

chapter three

Some Problems
of Assessment
and Measurement

Subsequent to Galton's pioneer conclusion that people differ in a systematic way in a variety of dimensions, psychologists have attempted to measure those differences with increasing accuracy. Measurement is the application of numbers to data or events according to a standard set of rules.

In the understanding of individual differences and occupational behavior, psychologists use material from a number of different sources. Probably the most widely used source of information and decision-making material is the *interview*, in which an expert gathers a wealth of information and impressions. As a measurement device, the interview has not reached high levels of precision or accuracy, although recent refinements have improved the procedure. Interview schedules, which provide specific topics to be covered and specific types of probing questions to be used, have helped to standardize methods. Even more uniformity is achieved in the structured interview, in which virtually every question to be asked is programmed ahead of time. Thus, the general types of answers and their significance can also be standardized, so that each subject, applicant, or counselee is exposed to the same questions and is given the same opportunities. This technique assumes that a given stimulus has the same meaning to each respondent—an assumption that is open to some question. The interview will never be the ultimate measurement technique, largely because of interviewer differences; but its persistently widespread acceptance and use suggest that the interview will probably retain its role as a major means of assessment.

Questionnaires are another means of gathering information about individuals. These are forms that are completed by the people being studied and that have the advantage of permitting large numbers of people to be included in an investigation at relatively little investigator cost. As with any measure or instrument, particularly those depending on self-report, the question of truthfulness is an issue with questionnaires. There is evidence, nonetheless, that people are surprisingly honest in the reporting of personal information, even when something important, such as a job, may be at stake. Progress has been made in studying individual differences with data obtained from questionnaires.

Rating scales, in which a person is asked to place another person or his behavior on a scale, are widely used, especially in personnel psychology. This method has the appearance of great objectivity; however, the construction of accurate, reliable rating scales is an accomplishment not very often realized because of limitations and variations in the people who construct them.

These methods of securing and organizing information about individuals, as well as personnel records, educational records, and essays or autobiographies, have all been widely incorporated in assessment procedures. The assessment and measurement techniques in which the greatest advances have been made, and to which most attention has been directed, are psychological tests.

To Test or Not to Test

Not every assessment situation calls for psychological tests, as seen by the popularity of other methods. There are times when what is needed is a confidential conference with a personnel man or time to discuss feelings and attitudes about a job with a professional counselor. There are cases in which the situation requires data other than those obtainable by tests. There are situations that are not complicated enough to warrant the trouble and expense of testing. In any of these situations, something other than testing is the appropriate approach to assessment and measurement.

Psychological tests are indicated when the questions to be asked have been thought through and when specific answers can be helpful. Carefully delimited questions and answers are possible only in well-defined situations, and for this reason it sometimes appears that psychological tests seek to know more and more about less and less. It is for this reason also that competent test users ask difficult questions of management, such as "What is it important to know about a candidate for this job?" To understand current problems in the use of tests, some background may be helpful.

A Bit of Background on Psychological Tests

Psychological tests are a product of applying basic knowledge about human behavior and its appraisal to a practical situation. They sample behavior to predict behavior. In most cases, tests have arisen from a need or from a question that required an answer. Questions such as "Which students will profit from the regular educational programs?" or "What men are likely to do well in pilot training?" have served as starting points for significant test developments. Around the turn of the century, the authorities in the French schools were faced with the problem of receiving more school-age children than they could handle and with the necessity of identifying children who would not profit from regular schooling. These authorities turned to Alfred Binet, who, with his associate Thomas Simon, developed the first standardized test of intelligence. Reasoning that children should learn certain things by the time they reached school age, Binet selected tasks from everyday experience (e.g., recognizing a common coin) and determined their level of difficulty by finding out how many children of a given age did, in fact, possess that kind of knowledge. As a means of identifying retarded children, this method was successful. It has served as the basis for one of the most widely used individually administered tests of intelligence, the Stanford-Binet, developed in its American form by Lewis Terman.

Group tests of intelligence came into being during World War I. Experiences with group tests of ability then led to a widespread over-optimism about what tests could do. As time passed and evidence accumulated from schools, colleges, industry, and government, initial claims were moderated and a more realistic attitude about tests prevailed.

In the 1930s, tests were improved and the use of testing increased, particularly in the assessment of aptitudes and interests relevant to occupations. Since, at that time, great numbers of men were out of work, the need to understand individual factors in obtaining and keeping a job, in maintaining or developing employability, was of paramount concern.

World War II presented another challenge to the satisfactory matching of men and jobs. With the tremendous demand for large numbers of men and women in various military specialties and in war industries, personnel testing again was emphasized as an instrument of national policy.

Again, the testing program of the war years not only provided for the more efficient immediate use of resources, but also provided a good foundation for postwar approaches to problems of manpower deployment and human readjustment. The major advances of World War II testing programs are reflected in multi-aptitude test batteries, which today are widely used in the selection and classification of men for jobs.

The use of tests in a wide range of programs has led to concern about the effects of these programs. Not only have aptitude tests played an increasingly important role in education, especially in ability grouping and in decisions of college admission, but testing in connection with occupational guidance and selection has also increased greatly. The results of such testing programs have generally been favorable when used with people who believe they have a chance to compete in society—for example, urban whites, Orientals, and Jews. Instead of inappropriately excluding individuals of low socioeconomic status from opportunities, tests have done much to make opportunities available to larger numbers of more diverse people with appropriate abilities (42).

As typically standardized, tests have not, however, worked so well with people who are traditionally disadvantaged, specifically with blacks. Therefore, with the increased emphasis on testing in a greater variety of contexts, testing programs have attracted criticism. The attacks have varied from reasonable observations of the correctable shortcomings of tests or test programs to emotional condemnations of all testing. A more useful question, then, is not really "To test or not to test?" but "What is the role of testing in our program?"

The Development of Tests

From the first question about personal qualities and school or job performance to the final production of a test to measure earlier behavior tendencies relevant to the later predicted behavior is a long and usually trying time. The steps in constructing a vocational test constitute a necessary sequence of decisions and events. A list of major steps in the development of a vocational test is as follows:

1. Job analysis
2. Selection of traits to test
3. Selection of criteria of success
4. Item construction and analysis
5. Standardization (obtaining distributions of scores from samples of appropriate subjects)
6. Validation (demonstrating that the test works in appropriate new situations)

This list includes all of the necessary steps, from the time a question is first formulated in the mind of an interested person to the time that a test is actually constructed and tried. In general, two approaches to test construction have been used to characterize the development of tests. These are the rational and the empirical approaches.

The *rational* approach is so named because the important preliminary step is a logical analysis of a situation, with an explanation couched in theoretical terms. For example, if we are interested in predicting how well a person will do in school, and if our theory describes learning ability as a composite of different skills and talents, then the kind of test we will develop will contain items sampling a wide range of such behaviors. If, on the other hand, we are concerned with a narrow definition of intelligence and we feel that this type of intelligence is appropriate for the prediction of the important aspects of school performance, then the test developed will contain primarily types of items measuring such ability.

The *empirical* approach begins with a consideration of the characteristics of people who behave in the ways under investigation. Usually a variety of items is written or collected and then administered to selected groups, and those items that differentiate the groups are retained in the test. Thus, whether or not an item is left in a test depends on its empirical discriminatory power. This criterion has both advantages and disadvantages. On the one hand, all of the items in the test have demonstrated relevance to the behavior in question. On the other hand, some of the items may not make sense in any way except that they were effective in one situation; they may not fit any existing theory. By way of contrast, items in rationally developed tests have interpretability since they were developed from a particular theoretical framework. For that reason, they may be expected to make sense in other situations.

A complete story of the development of a test must include both approaches. Even the most rationally initiated test rests on empirical evidence for its refinement and final validation, and all empirically developed tests rest on some theoretical foundation, even if that foundation is only implicit. It has been suggested that ideal test construction begins with a pool of rationally developed items, from which only those with supporting empirical relationships will be included. In this way, the advantages of both approaches would be gained, and the disadvantages of both approaches would be minimized.

Types of Tests

With numerous tests existing and with more being released annually, there is obvious need for categorization. Tests can be classified in a variety of ways. One typology, suggested by Lee Cronbach (23), will be mentioned here because of its special relevance to occupational psychology. Cronbach suggested that psychological tests could be meaningfully categorized as measures of maximum performance and as measures of typical performance.

Maximum performance measures are used to determine how well a person can do. Measures of this kind are usually ability tests, such as scholastic-aptitude tests or tests of mechanical ability. When these tests are given, the expectation is that the person will do as well as he can; he is often instructed to work as rapidly and accurately as possible. Everything is directed so that the individual will make the best possible scores. Later in the book, the relationship of tests of intelligence and special aptitudes to occupations will be explored.

Typical performance measures are directed more toward how a person is likely to act in various situations. In these kinds of tests, there are no "right" or "wrong" answers; rather, a person answers in terms of how he usually acts. The objective is not to get as good a score as possible, but rather to get an accurate picture of the person's genuine tendencies. Such measures are found in tests of interests, values, attitudes, and the like. These tests, in that they tell us how a person is likely to behave, also are of relevance to occupational psychology.

Some Psychometric Characteristics of Tests

In order to be able to use tests and measurements effectively, it is necessary to understand some of the characteristics of the instruments. Regardless of the particular type of test in question, there are some common features that they all share. Three such aspects are the distribution of test scores, validity, and the reliability of the test.

DISTRIBUTION

On any given measure of performance, whether it is the time needed to run 100 yards or how many vocabulary words a person knows, differences among individuals are expected. In a great many measurements, the scores people make are distributed in a bell-shaped manner, with most scores clustered around the middle. This is the famous "normal" curve, which has been found in measures such as height, weight, and intellectual ability. This curve, shown in Figure 3–1, is the basis for many statistical treatments, which often assume that perfectly accurate data would result in a normal curve.

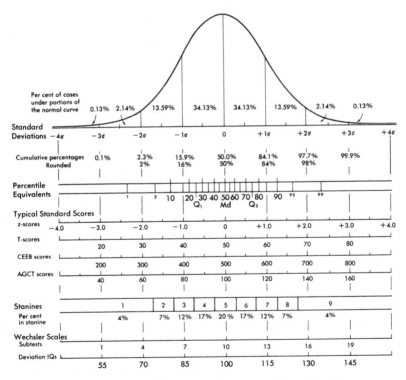

FIGURE 3–1. *The normal curve. Reproduced from the* Test Service Bulletin *of The Psychological Corporation, New York, N.Y.*

Data on the distribution of test scores in an appropriate sample of subjects are necessary for the interpretation of any one score. The *central tendency* of a distribution—in other words, the extent to which the scores cluster in the middle—is described in measures such as mean, median, or mode. In addition to knowing such average scores, it is necessary to know about the *dispersion* of the scores. Measures of dispersion include the range (lowest and highest scores made), the quartiles (scores at the 25th, 50th, and 75th percentiles), and the standard deviation (a summary measure of dispersion around the mean). Without these facts, it is impossible to interpret an individual's score. Knowing the distribution or how the scores on a test fall gives some idea of what a particular score means.

VALIDITY

The characteristics of a test should be known to be satisfactory through data that show an adequate range and variance. Thus, the test must be neither too hard nor too easy (if it is a measure of maximum performance), and there must be adequate variability (if it is a test of typical performance). After these conditions are met, the next questions are: What does the test measure? To what is it related? What does it predict?

The validity of a test depends on its relationships to significant behavior. A test is not simply "valid" or "invalid"; rather, it is valid or invalid for specific situations or applications. This fact is often forgotten in the use of tests, especially with those that aim to measure intelligence. Therefore, it is easy to attach too much importance to an IQ, making it more than just one global measure of general intellectual ability. The measure of a person's ability depends on the test given and the group to which he is compared. It is current practice to consider three separate kinds of validity: (1) content validity, or how well a test samples the kinds of behavior it is seeking to test, (2) criterion validity, or how well a test relates to other external measures, and (3) construct validity, or how relevant the test seems to be, theoretically and empirically, to accepted psychological constructs.

RELIABILITY

Another characteristic of a test sometimes confused with validity is reliability, which refers to the consistency or the stability of the test. All measures are subject to random influences that have nothing to do with the characteristic being measured. To the extent that these influences affect the scores obtained on a measure, the test is unreliable. As with validity, there are different ways of measuring the concept, but, in general, reliability is expressed in coefficients of the correlation between two measures. These measures are taken from the same test given at two different times, two different forms of the same test, or different parts of the same test (such as the odd-numbered items and the even-numbered items). Formerly, the technical guidelines for tests in psychology and education provided separate definitions for each kind of reliability, depending on the method used to compute it. Current practice does not always differentiate the kinds of reliability, although it is recommended that coefficients be given with an explanation of the formula used.

Difficulties in Test Taking

In the early days of psychological testing, relatively few people were involved in or affected by the use of test results. The good or bad that came from the tests was limited to those few who took the tests and perhaps to their immediate families. As the popularity of testing has spread, and as the lives of more people are affected by these tests, the difficulties of test interpretation have become more apparent and more critical. With an estimated 100,000,000 ability tests taken every year (42), the question clearly becomes one of national importance, something beyond the interest or domain of only the psychologists. Some concerns of testing deal primarily with measurement issues, such as determining how accurately or honestly a person has responded to a test. Other more general concerns focus on the social implications of testing, such as invasion of privacy or the effects of disadvantage on test performance.

Response Sets

In taking psychological tests, some people reveal that they have an orientation that predisposes them to answer in a way that distorts their scores. Such tendencies are called response sets; they may be conscious or the person may be unaware of them. Included in this category are conscious attempts at distortion (faking), tendencies to agree or say "yes" to questions (acquiescence), and tendencies to give typical approved answers (social desirability).

FAKING

When a person deliberately attempts to distort his answers on a test, he is said to be faking. This can be done with the idea of making oneself look better, healthier, or more flexible. It is difficult, however, to "fake good" on a test of ability, for it is hard to make a score significantly better than one deserves on well-constructed tests of ability. On the other hand, there are occasions on which a person does not want to look his best. In some military testing, some men have at times thought that it was not to their advantage to make the best possible score; therefore, they would "fake bad" on tests. Similarly, when a person applies for psychotherapeutic help, he may seek to make himself look as bad as possible in order to make the most persuasive case for receiving assistance.

Faking poses different problems for the different kinds of psychological tests. In tests of ability, faking can be a problem when a person wishes to make himself look less able than he is. Faking good on an ability test is not a problem unless cheating occurs, and prevention of cheating should be under the control of the test administrator. With inventories of interest or preferences, there are usually few problems of faking in counseling centers. The customary purpose of such centers is to assist the individual in his own decision making. In such cases, the counselee wants to have the best possible data; therefore, he makes an effort to answer the inventories honestly. It has been shown, however, that these interest tests can be faked: a person can make his interests appear more like those of people in certain occupations if he so desires. This possibility is one of the reasons that interest inventories are not widely used in selection, when the persons taking the tests may be strongly motivated to distort their responses.

In other personality inventories, faking can be an important source of inaccuracy. In order to detect such faking, a number of methods have been developed, which are quite successful in pointing out such behavior, even if faking cannot be entirely prevented. Some tests have consistency measures, which reflect the care and attention given in taking the test. Other tests have verification scores, which must be within a certain range for the scores to be seen as valid. Another means of detecting faking is the so-called "lie scale"; its items are answered in certain ways only by a very few people who have exceptionally good behavior and attitudes or by people who are lying. The problem of faking on psychological tests has not been completely solved, but definite progress has been made in the identification and understanding of faking.

ACQUIESCENCE

Some individuals have a tendency to agree, to answer "yes" to almost any question put to them; these people are said to be acquiescent. The opposite reaction is to be negativistic, denying or resisting any topic mentioned. Either of these tendencies can distort the answers given to a psychological test. For this reason, constructors of measurement instruments make an effort to develop balanced questionnaires and tests that are not affected in one direction or the other by these kinds of characteristics in individuals. Such distortion may or may not be conscious within the individual; he may or may not be aware that he tends to respond in that way.

SOCIAL DESIRABILITY

Most people usually respond in the manner that is socially accepted, in a manner that they believe will be approved. This tendency was known long before serious attempts were made to measure it and to control it. Allen Edwards (28) paid special attention to this particular response set in the development of his Personal Preference Schedule. When using forced-choice items, in which a person has to choose one or the other of two alternatives, Edwards matched items on the basis of their social desirability. By using items that had been rated as equivalent on social desirability, he believed that he had eliminated that source of bias in his results. That is, subjects would not choose one or the other alternative primarily on the basis of social desirability, since the two choices were equal on that dimension.

Whether or not this procedure does eliminate the effects of social desirability has been questioned by later evidence, making further steps necessary for these effects to be controlled. Because social desirability is such an important determinant of most people's interpersonal behavior, some psychologists now consider it a significant part of a person's behavior pattern, instead of the result of error in personality measurement. Whatever the outcome of the study of social desirability, Edwards and those who have followed him have provided another means for insight into behavior. Test developers are now less likely to construct items that are extreme in social desirability or undesirability.

Invasion of Privacy

In recent years, there has been an upsurge of resistance to psychological testing, much of it centered around the argument that tests often involve an invasion of privacy. It is widely held that each individual has the right not to reveal any more of himself than he chooses and that in some psychological tests he may unwittingly reveal personal information that he would want to keep to himself if he could make a conscious choice. The volume of protest at one point became such that, in 1965, Congressional hearings were held on the subject, leading to the limiting of the use of certain kinds of tests in federal personnel selection. Psychologists, writers, private citizens, public administrators, and other interested parties testified before hearings in both the House of Representatives and the Senate (4).

Of special relevance to occupational psychology was the fact that the major objection to tests was related to their use in selection and placement. There was little quarrel with the use of personality tests for diagnostic purposes or for helping disturbed people. Rather, the complaint most often registered was against the use of these tests in occupational decisions such as hiring and promoting. Most people feel that they know whether and why they should or should not be hired, and there was great resistance to including the personal information covered by some tests in these kinds of decisions.

The issue of invasion of privacy by psychological tests is not one that can be easily resolved. One expert in testing has suggested that two major considerations in the protection of privacy are relevance and informed consent (6). To be legitimate, psychological testing must ask the individual to reveal aspects of himself that are relevant to the objectives of the testing. One way to ensure such relevance is to use only tests that have been validated against the specific criterion under investigation. The other consideration, informed consent, refers to the agreement by the individual, after having been adequately informed of the nature and purpose of the testing, to participate in it.

Long before the controversy about the invasion of privacy, psychologists had developed standards of ethics to deal with this and other problems (3). The hearings and the recent attempts to come to grips with this topic, such as the publication of reports on privacy and behavioral research, have made evident the complicated nature of the issue and the need for continuing awareness of personal rights.

The Disadvantaged

Psychological tests use as their content the products of a culture, and they find their greatest usefulness within the culture in which they were developed. With renewed recognition of the plight of certain minority groups, most notably blacks, Puerto Ricans, and Appalachian whites, and with increased public and private effort to improve their condition, the usefulness of tests with such persons has been questioned. Is it fair to assess individuals who have had different backgrounds with the same instruments and standards? Can minority group members be expected to do as well as those who have had social privilege? Is there any appropriate way to take into account the special circumstances of some groups?

Psychological tests have been used to support arguments for the status quo and conclusions that are no longer considered valid, as well as to support desirable change and conclusions that seem both scientifically and socially more sound. For example, proponents of white supremacy have interpreted the differences between the intelligence-test scores of whites and those of Negroes as support for their position. Knowledge of the effects of environment on the development of intelligence makes such simple evidence insufficient for a scientifically valid explanation of the observed intellectual capacities of ethnic groups. Further studies of the intelligence of deprived groups reared under varying conditions have demonstrated the effects, detrimental or beneficial, that environment can have on performance on measures of intellectual capacity.

The fact remains that, on many measures of ability, individuals from deprived backgrounds do less well than do people who come from intellectually stimulating and socially mobile home situations. As measures of past performance and as predictors of future performance, tests accurately reflect existing environmental conditions. Children from deprived homes are not likely to do as well as are those who come from environments that provide stimulation to achieve and rewards for achieving in intellectual and academic endeavors. Because tests point out the resulting injustices without solving the problems, it is easy to blame the tests for the difficulties. On reflection, however, it is obvious that the fault is not appropriately ascribed to the measurement instrument that highlights a condition, but to citizens who permit the existence of conditions that have detrimental effects on the minds and lives of underprivileged people, or to those who misuse otherwise good instruments.

It has been suggested that tests be adjusted so that the differences between the disadvantaged and the privileged would be eliminated. To modify the content with this objective has been shown, however, to eliminate the very strength of the tests. A disadvantage in test taking is a disadvantage at work (6). Rather than changing the tests, thereby making them less accurate and less sensitive to disadvantage and to the effects of disadvantage, society must put effort into the changing of the conditions. Special consideration is called for in the development of prediction data and in the development of cutting scores, the minimum below which candidates are to be rejected, for the interpretation of test results obtained from disadvantaged people. Having been deprived in the past, such people need something more than conventional treatment in the present. Even among the disadvantaged, cutting scores appropriate for one ethnic group may be discriminatory toward workers from different ethnic backgrounds (58). Separate validation of job-relevant tests for advantaged and disadvantaged groups can provide appropriate cutting scores for the latter, making it possible to estimate the probability of success on the basis of the relevance of the trait tested in disadvantaged persons.

Uses of Test Results

In occupational psychology, tests have had their greatest value in two different processes: selection and counseling. The tests are often the same for both purposes, but the perspectives and the uses of tests in these processes are different.

Selection

Personnel selection seeks to maximize human resources by the most advantageous choice of workers for employment and the most effective placement of workers in jobs. The perspective is that of the job in which the worker is to be placed. The purpose of intelligent selection is the long-term benefit of the organization. In the selection of salesmen, for example, a company needs men who can make not only initial sales, but also repeat sales, of a product. The best selection is that which eventuates in the best continuing production and profit of the corporation.

Selection in an organization takes place at three levels: selection, placement, and advancement. First, *selection* refers to the decision to employ or not to employ an applicant. Second, when an individual is chosen, the new worker's position is determined through *placement*. This second step requires knowledge of differential human characteristics and their job relevance; it is a refinement of the simpler, more basic step of selection. Finally, within the organization, there is another process, *advancement* or upgrading, in which employees are promoted to higher-level positions. These different processes make use of tests in different ways. The questions of job behavior are different and require their own application of test data. Chapter 8 deals with these topics.

Counseling

The purposes of counseling are to assess a person's potential and to assist him in developing it in ways appropriate for him and for society's needs. Tests, as used in counseling, provide data on aptitudes, knowledge, interests, values, and personality traits. Such data help the individual to make decisions that are sound for himself as a person and as a member of society. Tests used in selection have been more thoroughly studied and developed than those used in counseling, so that we know more about the effectiveness of tests in selecting employees than in helping people choose occupations. Goldman (41) differentiates the uses of tests in counseling according to their informational and noninformational purposes.

INFORMATIONAL PURPOSES

One of the contributions of psychological tests is to provide information that may not otherwise be immediately available in counseling. Before counseling begins, psychological tests can help identify an individual's concern. That is, frequently a person has a vague discontent, and at such times test data can help in defining issues or the nature of a difficulty. Knowledge about the severity of the concern can also be of use in the precounseling diagnostic stage.

During counseling, test data such as aptitude and interest scores can assist in decisions to be made by the counselor and client. For the counselor, test data can be of help in selecting the techniques and methods that will be most effective for a particular client. Tests also can provide data desired by the counselee.

Finally, in regard to the most important aspect of counseling—

the person's behavior after counseling—Goldman discussses relating information to the client's postcounseling decisions. Among the uses of test data at this stage are the suggestion or identification of possible courses of action, the evaluation of alternatives and probable outcomes, and the judging of the suitability of tentative plans. Test data can also provide information for use in self-concept clarification and development.

NONINFORMATIONAL PURPOSES

The uses of test data are not limited to supplying specific information, although this may be the most popular use of tests in counseling. The benefits of test results are not necessarily limited to the facts themselves. Rather, there is often some value in the thinking that a test stimulates or provokes in a person. Some fields of work, for example, are never considered by a person because he is not familiar with them. Yet, if he is given a good test of interests, he may find that his similarity to men in those kinds of jobs is great enough for them to merit special thought.

Not all individuals who seek counseling are ready to get involved in a relationship that involves extended and frank discussion with the revelation of feelings and values. Therefore, counseling as a meaningful approach to problems is not readily accepted by everyone, even though the readiness to seek and use information may be there. For these people, test data can help serve as part of the groundwork for later counseling. Ideas may be introduced for later discussion or for consideration outside the counseling setting.

Counseling is sometimes characterized as a learning opportunity that provides experience in decision making. Though the particular facts presented on test profiles may not be crucial, sometimes counseling provides practice in decision making, in the integration of new information about oneself. Chapter 9 contains a more extensive treatment of the use of tests in counseling.

Summary

In the study of individual differences and occupational behavior, psychologists use material from different sources such as interviews, questionnaires, and rating scales. Measurement is the assignment of numbers to objects or characteristics according to a set of rules, and, in applied psychology, measurement has led to the development of psychological tests that are standard samples of behavior yielding data about an individual. Tests have often been the product of an attempt to solve a real educational or industrial problem—for example, deciding which students will profit from special classes. The development of a test involves both formulating a rational or theoretical basis and gathering empirical data about the test scores. It is necessary to know something about the distribution of scores, the reliability, and the validity of a particular test in order to interpret the test scores adequately. Difficulties in using tests include conscious attempts to distort one's scores as well as response tendencies of which an individual may not be aware. Recently, the issues of the invasion of privacy through psychological tests and the possible unfairness of using psychological tests with disadvantaged persons have become more prominent. In selection, test data can be helpful in decisions about hiring a prospective employee, placing him in a position that is right for him, and determining whether he should be promoted. In counseling, test data can provide such information as how a person's aptitudes compare with those of others like him. Test data can also be useful in stimulating a person's thinking, as in suggesting occupational alternatives that he may not have considered.

part two

Psychological Bases of
the Division of Labor

"Division of labor" means that society has evolved to the point at which it is not necessary for everyone to do everything for himself in order to survive. Initially, labor was divided primarily according to physical capacity, with intellectual and social ability playing secondary roles. Those who were able performed the tasks demanded of them by the environment and lived, while those who were not so physically endowed usually did not survive. Gradually life became less directly dependent on the physical environment, so that social and individual factors became more important. Specialization according to crafts (objects made or services rendered) came into existence with organized society. With the coming of the Industrial Revolution, it became more profitable than it had been for earlier economies to have some individuals concentrate on certain parts of a job while others carried out other parts of the same manufacturing process. Later, this approach was logically extended in what came to be known as mass production. In this system, each person is given a specialized, limited part of a process so complex that he could not carry it all out by himself.

Even before work was organized so that many individuals repeatedly performed the same limited task in relatively standardized situations, it was known that some men were better at some activities than at others. The question "Why does one person perform a particular task better than another person?" is basically a psychological question. For a variety of reasons, some individuals evidence more ability or greater preference for certain tasks while others excel at other tasks, and some excel at many tasks while others excel at none. These differences remain the basis for *occupational psychology*, which attempts to understand the relationship between the individual as a person and the occupational role which he plays.

Psychological concepts vary in degree of clarity and explicitness. Some psychological characteristics or traits are simply the product of a common-sense way of looking at things. The common-sense attitude explains, to a certain extent, why everyone is his own psychologist in the same way that everyone is his own philosopher. The similarity between common-sense constructs and psychological constructs has both advantages and disadvantages. On the one hand, some ideas, such as "intelligence" or "attitudes," can be understood with little further definition; on the other hand, the use of the same term to mean one thing in everyday conversation and something more precise in psychological literature can produce confusion. In order to minimize confusion, psychologists often devote considerable attention to definitions delimiting the concepts they use. For a concept to be useful in psychological research and literature, essential first steps are a clear definition of it and a set of operations for observing or measuring it in ways which can be understood and used by other investigators.

Part II of this book discusses the division of labor in relation to concepts of ability, motivation, interests, and other personality characteristics. The basic questions in regard to these concepts are: Can a person learn the principles or master the skills necessary to perform a job? Will he be attracted to a job strongly enough to master it and continue to work successfully at it? Does he care enough about the job itself or the rewards of the job to master it? Will he be comfortable associating with those who do similar work and identifying with them? Will he choose the occupation? Will he be chosen for it? Will he adapt to it? These types of questions are dealt with in considering the psychological bases of the division of labor.

chapter four

Occupational
Ability and
Aptitude
Patterns

Ability and aptitude generally refer to a person's capacity to learn or master material. The term "ability," however, often denotes skill acquired through education or experience, whereas the word "aptitude" is used exclusively to denote capacity to learn. The uses and measurement of aptitude are better understood than are its origins and development. Currently held explanations of aptitude development recognize that all individuals are endowed with varied potentials for developing certain behavioral characteristics and that the way in which these characteristics develop is largely dependent upon the environment in which the person is reared. As is the case with many other psychological and sociological variables, it is impossible to isolate the separate effects of heredity and environment in the development of aptitude because of their interaction on the organism.

Initially, the capacity to learn was considered to be a unitary entity, relatively straightforward and simple in nature. A person was able to learn or he was not able to learn. As more was understood about aptitudes, it became increasingly clear that while there may be a generalized capacity for learning, the level of ability exhibited by a person is largely dependent upon the subject matter to be learned. We all know individuals who are extremely gifted in one area but very inept in other areas. One stereotype of the college professor is that of the man who grasps the intricacies of abstract relationships among intellectual concepts but floods his car when trying to get it started.

The early tests of aptitude, however, were directed not toward specific capacities but toward the measurement of a general capacity for learning, or intelligence.

Intelligence

Among psychological concepts, intelligence has a most impressive and well-authenticated history. In the last century, Francis Galton systematically noted differences in the ways and extents of learning exhibited by different men. Differences of these kinds were also measured by Alfred Binet when he studied the learning and educability of children. By World War I, enough was known about intelligence for the development of tests that could be easily administered to large groups. Scores on these measures were valuable in screening thousands of men for later military assignment.

The first major investigations focusing on the relationship between intelligence and occupation grew out of World War I, when it was necessary to screen and classify men according to their ability to learn. Among the most successful measures of this ability was the Army Alpha Examination, which later became the basis for the Army General Classification Test (AGCT) of World War II. The AGCT was made up of items dealing with vocabulary, arithmetic problems, and block counting. Although it was not initially presented as an intelligence test, the nature of the items and the correlations between this test and other measures of intelligence make the AGCT qualify as a valid intelligence test.

Tests in this tradition were used in World War I with thousands of men, between the wars, in World War II with several million men, and again during the cold and hot wars that followed. In these periods, there were investigations of the relationships between intelligence measures and occupational group membership, the most extensive study being that conducted by Stewart (85) after World War II.

The Army General Classification Test and Occupations: Stewart's Study

Beginning with a sample of 81,000 white enlisted men, Stewart grouped the men according to their civilian occupation. AGCT scores were computed for each occupation, providing medians, means, and standard deviations for each. The findings provided evidence on the distribution of intelligence among the occupations, and, more specifically, showed the relative standings of the occupations in the general learning ability measured by the AGCT. Some of the major findings

TABLE 4-1. *Occupational groups whose AGCT medians lie in each half-sigma interval from the mean of all the medians. Based on white enlisted men in machine records survey taken June 30, 1944.**

−2.5 σ 85.3	−2.0 σ 89.9	−1.5 σ 94.5	−1.0 σ 99.1	−.5 σ 103.7	Mean 108.3	+.5 σ 112.9	+1.0 σ 117.5	+1.5 σ 122.1	+2.0 σ 126.7	+2.5 σ 131.3
Teamster	Marine Fireman	Tractor Driver	Welder, Electric Arc	Not Elsewhere Classified	Carpenter, Heavy Construction	Switchboard Installer, Telephone and Telegraph, Dial	Bookkeeper, General	Writer	Accountant	
Miner	Laundry Machine Operator	Painter, General	Plumber	Machinist's Helper	Dispatcher, Motor Vehicle	Cashier	Chief Clerk	Student, Civil Engineering	Student, Mechanical Engineering	
Farm Worker	Laborer	Foundryman	Switchman, Railway	Foreman, Labor	Gunsmith	Stock Record Clerk	Stenographer	Statistical Clerk	Personnel Clerk	
Lumberjack	Shoe Repairman	Animation Artist	Machine Operator	Locomotive Fireman	Musician, Instrumental	Clerk, General	Pharmacist	Student, Chemical Engineering	Student, Medicine	
	Barber	Hospital Orderly	Student, High School, Vocational	Entertainer	Tool Maker	Radio Repairman	Typist	Teacher	Chemist	
	Jackhammer Operator	Baker	Hammersmith	Meat Cutter	Nurse, Practical	Purchasing Agent	Draftsman	Lawyer	Student, Electrical Engineering	
	Groundman, Telephone, Telegraph, or Power	Packer, Supplies	Student, High School	Student, High School, Vocational	Photographer, Portrait	Survey and Instrument Man	Chemical Laboratory Assistant	Student, Business or Public Administration		
	Section Hand, Railway	Sewing Machine Operator	Agricultural Mechanic	Cabinetmaker	Photolithographer	Physics Laboratory Assistant	Draftsman, Mechanical	Auditor		
		Truck Driver, Heavy	Airplane Engine Mechanic	Airplane Engine Mechanic	Rodman and Chainman, Surveying	Stock Control Clerk	Investigator	Student, Dentistry		
		Painter, Automobile	Blacksmith	Heat Treater	Airplane Fabric and Dope Worker	Manager, Production	Reporter			
		Hoist Operator	Welder, Acetylene	Fire Fighter	Multilith or Multigraph Operator	Boilermaker, Layer-Out	Tool Designer			
		Construction Machine Operator	Bricklayer	Engineering Aide	Shipping Clerk	Radio Operator	Tabulating Machine Operator			
		Horsebreaker	Blaster or Powderman	Construction Equipment Mechanic	Printer	Linotype Operator	Addressing-Embossing Machine Operator			
		Tailor	Small Craft Operator	Optician	Steward	Student, Mechanics	Traffic Rate Clerk			
		Stonemason	Lineman, Power	Packer, High Explosives	Foreman, Warehouse	Salesman	Clerk-Typist			
		Crane Operator	Packing Case Maker	Petroleum Storage Technician	Bandsman, Cornet or Trumpet	Athletic Instructor	Postal Clerk			
		Upholsterer	Carpenter, General	Pattern Maker, Wood	Instrument Repairman, Non-electrical	Store Manager	Bookkeeping Machine Operator			
		Cook	Pipe Fitter	Electrician, Automotive	Boring Mill Operator	Installer-Repairman, Telephone and	Meat or Dairy Inspector			
		Concrete-Mixer Operator	Electric Truck Driver	Coppersmith	Projectionist, Motion Picture		Photographic Laboratory Technician			
		Truck Driver, Light	Highway Maintenance Man	Ship Fitter	Dental Laboratory Technician		Teletype Operator			
		Stationary Fireman	Automobile Serviceman	Sheet Metal Worker	Laboratory Technician, V-mail or Microfilm					
		Warehouseman	Rigger	Electroplater	Foreman, Machine Shop					
		Gas and Oil Man	Woodworking	Instrument Repairman, Electrical	Stock Clerk					
		Forging-Press Operator		Steam Fitter	Painter, Sign					
		Longshoreman		Diesel Mechanic	Machinist					
		Well Driller		Carpenter, Ship	Photographer, Aerial					
				Bandsman, Snare Drum						
				Lithographic Pressman						
				Electric Motor Repairman						
				Shop Maintenance						

Machine Operator	Mechanic	Engine Lathe Operator	Telegraph	Student, Sociology
Chauffeur	Job Pressman	Parts Clerk, Automotive	Motorcycle Mechanic	
Motorcyclist	Riveter, Pneumatic	Cook's Helper	Dispatcher Clerk, Crew	
Burner, Acetylene	Power Shovel Operator	Railway Mechanic, General	Tool Dresser	
	Photographic Technician, Aerial	Office Machine Serviceman	File Clerk	
	Brakeman, Railway	Student, High School, Commercial	Embalmer	
	Automobile Body Repairman	Electrician, Airplane	Brake Inspector, Railway	
	Tire Rebuilder	Student, Manual Arts	Airplane and Engine Mechanic	
	Utility Repairman	Policeman	Shop Clerk	
	Boilermaker	Sales Clerk	Artist	
	Foreman, Automotive Repair Shop	Electrician	Band Leader	
	Salvage Man	Lineman, Telephone and Telegraph	Photographer	
	Structural Steel Worker	Watch Repairman	Geologist	
	Welder, Combination	Receiving or Shipping Checker	Airplane Engine Service Mechanic	
	Welder, Spot	Car Mechanic, Railway	Cable Splicer, Telephone and Telegraph	
	Seaman	Toolroom Keeper	Surveyor	
	Engineman, Operating	Refrigeration Mechanic	Student, High School, Academic	
	Foreman, Construction	Cameraman, Motion Picture	Blueprinter or Photostat Operator	
	Millwright	Telephone Operator		
		Hatch Tender		

* Adapted from Naomi Stewart, AGCT scores of Army personnel grouped by occupation. Occupations, 1947, 26, 5-14. Reprinted by permission of the American Personnel and Guidance Association.

from the Army study are shown in Table 4–1, which is adapted from the Stewart article.

HIERARCHY

The first conclusion readily drawn from the AGCT data is that occupations arrange themselves in a hierarchy or rank order. Some of the differences between occupations are small (e.g., the difference between teamster and marine fireman, or between writer and accountant). The medians of the two occupations in such cases are so similar that it is possible or even probable that another sampling of the occupations would produce different results. Still, there are many differences between occupations that are quite definite, large, and clear—that is, statistically significant (e.g., the difference between tractor driver and bookkeeper). It is not likely that another sampling of these occupations would produce a difference in their relative positions in the list. Thus, we can conclude that occupations can be arranged in a meaningful hierarchy based on intelligence or ability to learn.

Comparison of the World War II data with results obtained during and after World War I revealed the relative temporal stability of the occupational hierarchy. The Stewart (85) medians correlated .87 with those of Bridges (113) and .84 with those of Fryer (36). There were differences between the medians of some specific occupations at these different times, but the general picture remained the same. The men of World War II seemed to score higher than those of World War I; this can perhaps be attributed to the rise in the general educational level of American men and the general rise in the technology of twentieth-century America.

DISTRIBUTION

A second conclusion to be drawn from the AGCT data is that, in the total sample, the occupations tend to cluster in the middle, with few occupations at the extremes. When the median or middle scores of each occupation are placed on the scale, they tend to fall in a distribution that is almost normal in shape. (A "normal" curve is the bell-shaped curve that is found frequently in representations of physical and psychological characteristics.) If the occupational medians had been distributed horizontally in a "flat" curve, approximately the same number of occupations would have appeared at each level.

This topic refers to the way in which scores are spread around the average score. Within the total sample, it is seen that the occupations have median scores that are above and below the mean (average) of these medians. In a similar way, within each occupation, the scores of the individuals vary around the median for that particular occupational group. Occupations with high median scores (e.g., personnel clerk or civil engineering student) tend to have less variability than do those with low median scores (e.g., miner or laundry machine operator). Some of this difference in variation may be explained by the entrance requirements of the occupations: certain occupations, especially those with high medians, can be entered only by demonstrating a high level of ability in training. Among the lower-level occupations, there are no such hurdles to overcome. People can enter and leave these occupations with considerable ease. In some low-median occupations there are individuals who could qualify for *any* occupation, if the question of aptitude were the only one considered.

OVERLAP

In light of the clear evidence that there is an intellectual hierarchy of occupations, it is easy to forget the wide range of intelligence in a given occupation and the considerable overlap between occupations. While it is possible to determine an average score for an occupation, it is almost impossible to establish a ceiling score for a given occupation. Regardless of the functional requirements of a job, there are high-scoring men in almost every occupation. For these and other reasons such as the dependence of standards on supply and demand, the medians and distributions of ability scores are considered loose guidelines, rather than absolute facts about the ability levels of specific occupations.

Aptitudes

The data from the Army studies established an occupational hierarchy based on a single test of overall intelligence. It has been noted earlier, however, that ability is more complex than a unitary construct. Individuals have varied levels of talent in different areas. That is, people learn some things more quickly than they learn other things, but there is a tendency for those who learn one activity fast to learn other things rapidly too. People are not uniformly fast or slow in all areas, however. In order to determine the relationship between aptitudes and occupations, several multiple-aptitude test batteries have been used to study occupational performance. Some outstanding examples of this approach are described below.

The General Aptitude Test Battery (GATB): Work of Shartle and Dvorak

The relationship between aptitudes and occupations has been a concern of the United States Employment Service (USES) since the economic depression that preceded World War II. Building on work done at the University of Minnesota in the 1930s (73), the USES has conducted a long-term, systematic study of aptitudes and job performance (81, 26, 8). This research has been based on two primary assumptions: (1) that aptitude tests can be reduced to a few important underlying factors, and (2) that occupations can be grouped according to the aptitudes required.

THE TEST BATTERY

The general philosophy of the USES in test construction has been to follow the pattern of previously successful aptitude tests. In general, the more successful aptitude tests have been concerned primarily with empirical (occupational) results, rather than striving for theoretical (factorial) purity. Selecting test items from previous tests and developing its own new items, the USES produced 12 aptitude tests, which were combined to measure nine different aptitudes: (1) G—Intelligence, (2) V—Verbal Aptitude, (3) N—Numerical Aptitude, (4) S—Spatial Aptitude, (5) P—Form Perception, (6) Q—Clerical Perception, (7) K—Motor Coordination, (8) F—Finger Dexterity, and (9) M—Manual Dexterity.

In order to standardize these tests—that is, to determine what scores should be expected from average workers—the USES selected 4,000 workers representative of the entire U.S. labor force. With this sample, the raw aptitude scores were converted to means of 100 with standard deviations of 20. The next step in the study of aptitudes and occupations was to determine how various occupations scored on these aptitude measures. Occupational norms were developed.

OCCUPATIONAL NORMS

The first step in establishing occupational norms for a particular occupation was *job analysis*. Such analysis was a thorough study of the job by observation and interviews, leading to tentative conclusions about the aptitudes needed in the performance of the duties of the occupation. Because the GATB sought to relate aptitudes to job performance, rather than simply to determine the ability levels of workers in particular occupations, judgments were needed about the level of performance. That is, it was necessary to establish criteria of performance in a given job. Merely holding the job was not accepted as adequate evidence of satisfactory performance. Instead, criteria were set up using both objective and subjective measures of job performance. The objective criteria characteristically were quantifiable, public aspects of a job, such as the number of assemblies completed or the number of rejected products. Subjective measures were based on less tangible aspects of an occupation and typically involved the judgment of a supervisor. On the basis of these judgments, workers were assigned to criterion groups of high and low performance.

After the job analysis and the selection of suitable criteria for a particular job, the entire GATB was administered to a sample of workers employed in that job. The next step was data analysis. The specific aptitudes included in the occupational norms were chosen in terms of importance to the occupation, a relatively small standard deviation, a relatively high mean score, and correlation with the criterion measures.

The establishment of occupational norms reflects the validated assumption that the aptitudes are indeed related to job performance. Based on the occupational distributions of aptitudes, cutoff points were established. These points were minimum requirements of the aptitudes for that particular occupation. Scores that fell at the level of, or higher than, the cutoff points were classified as qualifying scores, while those that fell below the minimum were considered nonqualifying. For an individual to achieve a qualifying score for a given occupation, he had to meet the minimums on *all* the aptitudes. A deficit in one area could not be compensated by a surplus of ability in another aptitude. For example, in the occupational norms, the cutoff points for Architectural Draftsman are G-95, N-90, S-110, and F-80. An individual presenting the aptitude scores of G-105, N-90, S-110, and F-90 (equal or superior to the cutting score on each relevant aptitude) would qualify for that occupation, whereas a worker whose scores were

G-90, N-95, S-115, and F-95 (below the cutoff on G and above on N, S, and F) would not have qualifying scores, even though his scores in three of the four aptitudes were above the cutoff points.

OCCUPATIONAL APTITUDE PATTERNS (OAP)

With the establishment of occupational norms on the GATB, it became possible to compare the aptitude requirements of different jobs. The occupational norms were based on the three or four aptitudes most important to a particular occupation. This method of comparing the abilities of individuals with occupational requirements, however, was still tedious because of the number of different occupations, each with its own score.

The constellations of occupational norms had similar patterns, and on the basis of these similar aptitude requirements, the USES introduced the *Occupational Aptitude Pattern* (OAP). An OAP was a set of three aptitude cutoff scores that were appropriate for a group of occupations. One OAP, then, could represent the aptitude requirements for an entire group of occupations. The OAP shown in Table 4-2 included minimum aptitudes for occupations such as accountant, pharmacist, and underwriter and had cutoff scores of 115 on Intelligence (G), 115 on Numerical Aptitude (N), and 105 on Clerical Perception (Q). Another OAP covered the aptitudes required for occupations such as carpenter, plumber, machinist, and sheet metal worker and had cutoff scores of 80 on Numerical (N), 90 on Spatial Aptitude (S), and 80 on Manual Dexterity (M) (26).

The first occupations were included in the OAP's because test data showed direct relationships between the OAP's and performance in those occupations. Later, other occupations were added on the basis of their similarity to each other as shown by job analysis in the absence of test and criterion data. With continuing study, the number of OAP's has risen to 35, covering several hundred different occupations.

CONCLUSIONS

From the GATB scores it can be seen that, if a comprehensive test battery is used and a diversity of occupational samples obtained, the relationship between aptitudes and occupations can be clarified. A summary article covering 424 studies, which involved over 25,000 employees, applicants, trainees, and students, has documented again the usefulness of the GATB in the prediction of performance in training or on the job (8). It may be helpful to review here the general findings from GATB results in the terms used in the summary of the AGCT study.

The hierarchy of occupations is clearly demonstrated in each of the specific aptitudes. Occupations can be ranked on the basis of levels of ability shown by the cutoff scores on each of the different aptitudes. For this reason, an individual with a given aptitude score could stand near the top of one group and in the lower end of the distribution in another group. For example, a person with a clerical-aptitude score of 110 would be among the most gifted in the sales clerk category, but at the same time he would rank lower than average among accountants.

TABLE 4–2. *Occupations included in one Occupational Aptitude Pattern (OAP) example.**

OCCUPATIONS	OAP CUTOFF SCORES		
	G-Intelligence 115	*N-Numerical* 115	*C-Clerical* 105
Laboratory Science Work			
Pharmaceutical Botanist			
Pharmacist	110	115	
Business Relations Work and Related			
Accountant, Cost			
Accountant, General	105	115	
Accountant, Public			
Accountant, Tax			
Accountant, Budget			
Auditor	105	115	
Accounting System Expert			
Statistician I			
Estimator			
Assessor			
Underwriter	120	115	105
General Recording Work			
Teller	105	110	105

* *General Aptitude Test Battery, Section II: Scoring Directions and Norms.* Washington: U.S. Department of Labor, 1958.

The distribution of special-aptitude scores is also similar to the distributions found for general aptitude (intelligence) in the AGCT data. As is the case with many psychological and physical variables, most of the occupations clustered around an overall mean, with few occupations at the extremes of much more aptitude or much less aptitude than the general average. The distributions themselves approximated the normal curve.

Variability was also a relevant factor in the GATB results. There had been no occupational selection on the basis of aptitudes that were apparently irrelevant to an occupation; consequently, there was wide individual variation. The extent of variation was a major consideration in the selection of aptitudes for the occupational norms and, indirectly, for the Occupational Aptitude Patterns. As with the AGCT results, occupations that required a high level of an aptitude tended to have smaller variances, or narrower distribution of scores.

Overlapping is a factor that cannot be overlooked in the GATB results. Although there is a definite hierarchy of aptitudes exhibited by the various occupations, and although the variance of aptitude scores tends to be restricted in proportion to the importance of the aptitude for the given occupation, there is considerable overlap in the aptitude levels required by different occupations. This overlap is illustrated by the similarities even among the various OAP's. An individual usually is capable of performing the duties and tasks of a wide variety of jobs: people are occupationally multi-potential. The actual job selected depends on much more than aptitude alone. Other considerations such as interests, personality, the supply and demand of manpower on the labor market, and the general economy are part of the decision made by a job seeker.

The specific relevance of aptitudes was the most important and impressive finding made evident by the GATB results. Not all aptitudes are required to a significant degree by all occupations. Some occupations require high levels of several aptitudes and less of others, whereas other occupations require high levels of other aptitudes. A broad scope of aptitudes was sampled by the GATB, and the Occupational Ability Patterns document the fact that specific aptitudes have meaning for specific types of occupations. These OAP's illustrate the similarities and differences among occupational aptitude requirements by expressing these requirements in standard terms. They reflect the varied demands of jobs and their specific aptitude requirements.

Ten Thousand Careers: Air Force Tests in the Thorndike and Hagen Study

Another major study of aptitudes and occupations was that of Thorndike and Hagen (101). These psychologists were interested in the relationship of aptitude scores to later occupational success, but their results also tell us something about the distribution of aptitudes among occupations.

During World War II, tests were administered by the Armed Forces to several million individuals. One service program that was particularly successful in overcoming problems of selection and classification of personnel by the use of tests was the Army Aviation Psychology Program. Thorndike and Hagen began their study with a sample of 17,000 aviation cadets tested under this program in 1943. The men had already been screened by a preliminary intelligence test and therefore represented a select group rather than the general population. A follow-up of these cadets was made 13 years later, in 1956, when the data on their postwar occupational behavior were gathered by questionnaire.

The Aviation Cadet Classification Battery was composed of 20 aptitude tests including reading, general information, numerical reasoning, spatial relations, psychomotor coordination, and other such aptitudes. Each test was directed toward the measurement of a specific aptitude; however, in the analysis of the results, it became clear that these separate tests could be combined and that the results could be meaningfully communicated in five composite scores. The final composite aptitudes scores were labeled: General Intellectual, Numerical Fluency, Visual Perception, Mechanical, and Psychomotor.

DISTRIBUTION

Inspection of the occupational rankings on these composite scores produced findings similar to those of the AGCT and the GATB. Occupations could be ranked in a definite hierarchy, with many occupations clustered around the middle. As one proceeded farther and farther from the middle, there were fewer occupations. Some occupations ranked either high or low on most aptitudes, as do some individuals. Most of the occupations, however, were higher in some aptitudes than they were in others.

RELEVANCE OF SPECIFIC APTITUDES

Occupations tended to rank highest on aptitudes that are logically related to the performance of the job. For example, on General Intellectual ability the highest scoring groups were chemical engineers, physical scientists, college professors, and civil engineers, while those highest on Numerical Fluency were treasurers, comptrollers, accountants, and auditors. High scorers on Visual Perception were architects and miners and drillers. High Mechanical aptitude was most evident among miners and drillers, airplane pilots, and mechanical engineers. High scorers on Psychomotor aptitude were miners and drillers and engine mechanics. Table 4–3, with lists adapted from Thorndike and Hagen, classifies occupations according to their highest ability scores.

TABLE 4–3. *Occupations classified according to their highest ability scores.**

HIGHEST ABILITY	OCCUPATION
General Intellectual	College Professors
	Dentists
	Engineers
	Lawyers
	Physicians
	Scientists
	Social Workers
Numerical Fluency	Accountants
	Office Managers
	Optometrists
	Painters
	Pharmacists
	Purchasing Agents
	Salesmen
	Treasurers, Comptrollers
Visual Perception	Advertising Agents
	Architects
	Draftsmen
	Printing Craftsmen
	Radio, TV Repairmen
Mechanical	Airplane Pilots
	Carpenters
	Crane Operators
	Electricians
	Engine Mechanics
	Farmers
	Sheet Metal Workers
Psychomotor	Firemen
	Guards
	Machinists
	Miners, Drillers
	Plumbers
	Service and Recreation Managers

* Adapted from Robert L. Thorndike and Elizabeth Hagen, *Ten Thousand Careers* (New York: Wiley, 1959), pp. 32–34. Used by permission.

The accountants' scores provide a good illustration of aptitude distribution *within* an occupational group. Accountants were highest in an aptitude relevant to their job, Numerical Fluency. They were relatively low in other aptitudes, such as Mechanical and Psychomotor, not clearly related to their occupation. Finally, the range of aptitudes exhibited by the accountants went from very low to very high, even on the aptitude most directly relevant to their work. Figure 4–1, taken from Thorndike and Hagen (p. 25), presents the medians and distributions of the accountants' scores.

In the words of these psychologists, the general conclusion in their study about aptitudes and occupations was that differences between occupational groups were "real, sometimes substantial, and, in most cases, sensible (p. 49)."

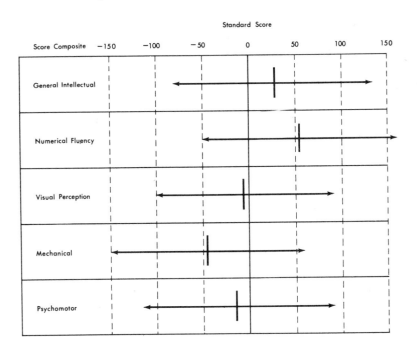

FIGURE 4–1. *Score Composite Means and Standard Deviations for 235 Accountants. Reprinted from Robert L. Thorndike and Elizabeth Hagen,* Ten Thousand Careers *(New York: Wiley, 1959), p. 25.*

Aptitude Tests and Occupations

The research on aptitude tests and the prediction of occupational performance has been summarized by Ghiselli (39) in a recent book, *The Validity of Occupational Aptitude Tests*. Psychological tests were grouped into measures of Intellectual Abilities, Spatial and Mechanical Abilities, Perceptual Accuracy, Psychomotor Abilities, and Personality Traits. The parallels between the categorization here and that used by Thorndike and Hagen are apparent. Test scores were related to performance in two areas: success in training and level of job proficiency.

For all jobs, Ghiselli found that success in training was accurately predicted by at least one kind of aptitude test, and usually by two or three kinds. Consistent with the results of the USES research, as well as those of Thorndike and Hagen, each of the different kinds of aptitudes was more closely related to some occupations than to others. The aptitudes most relevant usually were consistent with what would be expected from a logical analysis of the job. For example, success in clerical training was most accurately predicted by tests of Intellectual Abilities and Perceptual Accuracy, while for vehicle operators, success in training was most accurately predicted by Spatial and Mechanical abilities tests.

Success in training can be predicted better than level of job proficiency, as should be expected with the use of aptitude (ability to learn) tests. Ghiselli's conclusions bear out this difference in predictability. Predicting level of job proficiency involves a much more complicated situation for evaluation than does prediction in the training situation in which performance often can be defined simply as the degree to which assigned subject matter or skills have been learned. Even so, aptitude tests correlated moderately well with level of performance in some types of occupations. Intellectual Abilities, Perceptual Accuracy, and Personality Traits, for example, all predicted success in administrative positions moderately well. For job proficiency of sales clerks, Personality Traits gave the best predictions, whereas Intellectual Ability tests and Perceptual Accuracy were not so useful.

As in the development of the Occupational Aptitude Patterns, it was possible for Ghiselli to group occupations according to similarity of aptitude requirements. The three types of aptitude tests (Intellectual abilities, Spatial and Mechanical abilities, and Perceptual Accuracy) provided the basis for a three-dimensional classification system. (Psychomotor Abilities and Personality Traits could not be used as dimensions since these measures were too heterogeneous and varied.) In this way of looking at the data, the occupations fell into two main clusters, each with a number of sub-clusters. That is, there were two major patterns of aptitude requirements, with systematic variation in each of these patterns. The psychological requirements were not always obvious from the descriptions of the jobs: some occupations with apparently similar tasks, such as sales clerks and salesmen, required very different abilities, while some other apparently different occupations, such as sales clerks and service workers, required very similar abilities. This conclusion raises serious questions about the wisdom or soundness of the USES practice of adding occupations to OAP's on the basis of job analyses alone, without direct test data. At the same time, the variation in aptitude requirements shown in this kind of occupational grouping is another indication of the relevance of certain specific aptitudes for certain occupations and their irrelevance for certain others.

Aptitudes and Success

Aptitude is defined as the capacity to learn, while general aptitude or intelligence is defined as the capacity to solve problems using symbols. We have seen that the concept of general aptitude began as a relatively simple one, and that with the advance in test procedures and analyses, more and more separate kinds of abilities have been defined. Advances in this area are reflected in the increasing variety of tests measuring an ever-increasing number of aptitudes. We have seen that some aptitudes have special relevance for occupational behavior. After establishing the existence of aptitude patterns typical of occupations, the next logical question is: How do these aptitude measures relate to success in an occupation?

Definitions of Success

The concept of success has been taken from everyday language and has proved to be extremely difficult for psychologists to define and to measure. In occupational behavior, there are some definitions of success that are widely held and clear-cut. For example, in business a very *real* criterion of success is how much money a person makes. Still, few people would accept this as an *adequate* definition of success. This kind of criterion is inappropriate and out of place in some occupations, in which, for example, members renounce material possessions or view them as quite incidental to service to society, to the pursuit of knowledge, or to the creation of beauty. In addition to the difficulty in obtaining agreement about the relatively straightforward financial criterion of success, there is the fact that success in one field is difficult to compare with success in another occupational area. Who can say that a shop foreman is more successful or less successful in his work than a bookstore salesman is in his?

More perplexing than the confusions about success within an occupation or between different occupations is the complexity of the concept of success within each person. As has been noted many times, success is an individual matter. What others may regard as a real accomplishment an individual may regard as not really a good job. On the other hand, a person can feel a sense of pride and achievement in some part of his job that is not necessarily regarded as noteworthy by others. Differences between individual definitions of success are brought out in the questions: "What would wealth have been to Ghandi, or the love and respect of humble men and women to Bismarck? What use had Thoreau for prestige and status, or Theodore Roosevelt for opportunities to be alone with himself and the universe?" (90, p. 7).

Measures of Success

Some changes in emphasis in the measurement of occupational success can be illustrated by the variety of criteria that have been developed. World War I documented the need for reliable measures of vocational promise and capacity, and effective measures were developed from instruments that had their beginning at that time. After the war, the study of occupational success focused primarily on measures of earnings and output—that is, how much a worker produced. During the 1920s and 1930s, the concepts of advancement and stability were added to the study of success. Most of these measures were objective in that they minimized the individual judgment of the investigator. Later the concept of success was broadened to include supervisors' or co-workers' ratings of the worker's success. Finally, the feelings and perceptions of the worker himself are now an important consideration in the study of success.

Ratings as measures of success are usually thought of as subjective since they ask for individual interpretation and judgment in the basic data, but in numerical form, they often appear to be objective. The objective measures (earnings, output, stability) involve interpretation in the decision to use such data. Thus, there are really no purely objective or subjective measures of success, although it is useful at times to categorize measures in these terms.

As with many issues in vocational psychology, until recently success has been studied occupationally. That is, it has been studied in terms of how well a person is doing at a specific time in a type of work or in a specific position. A person's *occupation* is the major work activity in which he engages at a given time, while his *career* is his sequence of work activities or occupations over a period of time (a distinction dealt with in some detail in Chapter 6). With this differentiation, it becomes clear that in addition to the need for understanding occupational success, there is a need for understanding career success.

OCCUPATIONAL SUCCESS

Placement on the occupational ladder was the criterion in the first major study that investigated the relationship between intelligence and occupations, the Army study of World War I. That study and Stewart's (85) World War II study found that intelligence was related to occupations at least to the extent that there were hierarchies of intelligence, with some occupations clearly higher than others. The higher occupations tended to have a smaller amount of variation, probably reflecting the entrance requirements and the hurdles that individuals had to overcome in order to enter the jobs.

Success in a specific occupation was the focus of the later GATB studies, which attempted to provide a more systematic study of work performance and aptitudes. Not only were individuals grouped according to their jobs, but within jobs they were segregated into successful and less successful groups according to criteria such as output, supervisors' ratings, and performance in training. The basis for categorization is not always explicit in the GATB literature, and this lack of explicitness is a drawback because there may be a substantial difference between work performance as reflected in measures of output and ratings by supervisors. Even more substantial is the difference between performance in training and actual performance on the job. With more refined measures of work performance, however, the investigators using the GATB were able to find definite relationships between aptitude scores and work performance. Certain abilities were more relevant and important for certain jobs, and the amount of aptitude was indeed related to success in the work.

In the study for which the primary focus was the relationship between aptitude scores and later occupations, *Ten Thousand Careers* (101), the results in the prediction of degree of success in a specific occupation were essentially negative. But the criteria of success in this study were more varied and complex than those of the studies which preceded it. Some of the criteria were conventional measures of success in specific occupations, such as monthly earnings in dentistry or number of workers supervised in an accounting office, while other criteria would more appropriately be labeled measures of career success. The one criterion of success in an occupation that did show some significant relationships to aptitude was strikingly similar to the commonsense definition of success: monthly earnings. In addition, the relationships between occupational aptitudes and rank in the hierarchy of occupations and the occupational differentiating power of aptitude patterns constitute impressive evidence of a different kind of relationship between aptitude and success.

The Career Pattern Study, a long-term investigation of vocational behavior that has followed boys and young men from the eighth and ninth grades to their middle twenties and beyond, has differentiated between occupational success and career success. Occupational success is measured in terms of the occupational level attained, self-estimated occupational success, and the individual's perceptions of how well his assets are used and of the quality of his opportunities for self-expression. Moderate relationships have been found between these measures and intelligence (97).

CAREER SUCCESS

Occupational success is a reflection of how well a person is doing at a particular time in a particular type of work, while the study of career success involves the progress of an individual over an extended period of time, sometimes in a number of different positions. It is obvious that the prediction and study of career success is more complicated and involved. The Thorndike and Hagen Study, aptly named *Ten Thousand Careers,* was a study of both occupational success and career success in relation to ability or aptitude scores. Although it stressed occupational success, it missed the importance of the distinction between occupational and career success. Measures such as vertical mobility (how far a person has moved up or down the occupational ladder) and length of time in the occupation are more career than occupational in their orientation. These criterion measures had no significant relationship to the aptitude measures.

The Career Pattern Study investigated career success by focusing on the changes of position that a person makes. Measures of progress include consideration of changes in equity (what a person gains or loses in a move), the realism of reasons for a move, improvement or lack of improvement in the use of abilities and measured interests, progress toward a specific goal, improvement or lack of improvement in socioeconomic and educational level, and floundering or stabilizing vocational behavior. Finally, the career success of a person was studied in terms of a total score based on the separate factors that contribute to career success. Results of this study, some of which are discussed in Chapter 6, showed intelligence to be the variable that is most closely related to the career success measures of change in equity, realism for moves, and improvement in educational level. The summary measure of career success was also related to intelligence, as was the global judgment of stabilizing behavior. Another finding of interest was that career success was only mildly, but positively, related to occupational success. These two success concepts, in job and in career, are related to each other, although they are not the same thing.

SUCCESS AS OCCUPATIONAL MEMBERSHIP

Most studies of success take as their criterion one aspect of a worker's job performance. Some studies rely on supervisors' ratings of the worker; others take the more direct measures of the individual's performance such as the number of finished assemblies or other output units he completes per unit of time, the ratio of unsatisfactory to satisfactory products he turns out per day, or some other such quantifiable measure of job performance. Because of the limitations of these kinds of measures, and because of the difficulty in finding meaningful relationships between such measures and psychological concepts, it has been suggested that a better measure of success would be simply the person's occupational membership. That a person is able to keep on doing something is prima facie evidence of success in doing it.

In his studies of vocational interests, Strong (88) decided that if a person achieved entry into a given occupation and if he survived in that occupation for at least three years, he could be considered a success. Later, Strong expressed the opinion that five years might have been a better minimum. This kind of definition, of course, also has its drawbacks and its sources of inaccuracy. A person can survive in an occupation, maintained by family or social influence, without being considered a success by his peers or by himself. But these are no doubt exceptions in a competitive economy.

In spite of these and other difficulties with occupational membership as a criterion of success, it therefore remains as perhaps the most reliable, valid, and practical criterion. After lamenting difficulties in the *Ten Thousand Careers* study, Thorndike and Hagen concluded that occupational membership was in fact the only practical measure of success. Still, *within* a given occupation, there should be meaningful differentiations on degrees of success, and income within an occupation may be a reasonable measure of such success.

The Relationship between Aptitude and Success

A primary difficulty in relating aptitude to success seems to be in coming to grips with some acceptable definition of success. We are not entirely satisfied with our understanding of aptitude, but we know much more about it than we do about success. The relationship between occupational membership and aptitude seems now even more clear than it did at first: some occupations have higher average aptitude levels than do other occupations, and these levels and differences are quite stable over time.

The research on aptitude and success has been reviewed extensively by Roe (74), by Super and Crites (95), and by Crites (22). There have been no startling newer conclusions or discoveries; therefore, the general conclusions reached by Super and Crites remain valid.

1. People tend, in so far as circumstances permit, to gravitate toward jobs in which they have the ability to compete successfully with others.

2. Given intelligence above the minimum required for learning the occupation, be it executive work, teaching, packing, or light assembly work, additional increments of intelligence appear to have no special effect on an individual's success in that occupation. . . .

3. In routine occupations requiring speed and accuracy, whether clerical or semiskilled factory jobs, intelligence as measured by alertness rather than a power [untimed] test is related to success in the learning period and, in some vocations, after the initial adjustments are made [p. 99].

In concluding the discussion of aptitude and success, the findings summarized by Super and Crites, as well as those of Thorndike and Hagen and other investigators, all seem to be consistent with the use of critical cutting scores used by USES. The specific-hurdle approach seems to fit the real world. This approach, it will be recalled, assumes that an individual must possess certain minimum levels in relevant aptitudes in order to qualify for an occupation. Once a person has evidenced that he is gifted beyond that minimum, no statements are made about how well he should do in that occupation. Given the minimum ability for successful completion of training or for successful entry into that occupation, in most cases, additional ability is not related particularly closely to success. Success, defined as how far a person advances, how much he contributes to a field, or how much above average he is in that field, seems to be largely a reflection of personality characteristics such as interests, needs, self-concepts, and motivations, and of situational factors that are independent of the individual.

Aptitudes and Satisfaction

Given that a person has the ability to master a job and that he is able to gain entry into the job, the next logical question about aptitudes and job performance is: How do aptitudes relate to satisfaction with the job? Like success, satisfaction is an extremely individual matter, and the only one who can really tell whether or not a person is satisfied is the individual himself. Therefore, most of the attempts to study satisfaction have relied on simple verbal reports from workers themselves.

Although there are real similarities between satisfaction and success, and although knowing a person's satisfaction usually tells us something about his success and vice versa, the two concepts are actually separate, if not completely independent. The confusion between satisfaction and success is another example of the difficulties occupational psychologists become involved with when the terms they use are borrowed directly from everyday language. A British industrial psychologist, Alastair

Heron, proposed the term "satisfactoriness" to refer to the acceptability of a worker's performance to his employers, and the limitation of the term "satisfaction" to consideration of how the worker himself feels about his own situation.

Definitions of Satisfaction

There are many approaches to the study of satisfaction. The findings of research on satisfaction therefore depend, in part, on how satisfaction is measured. The most common method of determining a worker's satisfaction with his job has been to ask him, and the answers to such a question depend partly on how it is asked. Three types of questions have commonly been used. First is the direct question about satisfaction: "Do you like your job?" Second, the question is phrased: "If you had it to do again, would you choose your present occupation?" Finally, the third approach infers satisfaction from the workers' behavior. How workers feel about their jobs may be less well revealed by verbal behavior than by performance on their jobs.

DO YOU LIKE YOUR JOB?

Using this question and others essentially like it, Robert Hoppock (50) carried out a pioneer study of job satisfaction. Studying a national sample of teachers and the entire labor force of a small town in Pennsylvania and reviewing other studies, Hoppock was led to conclude that most workers, regardless of socioeconomic level, were relatively satisfied. There were, indeed, some expected differences in satisfaction, with workers at higher levels being more satisfied than those at the lower levels, but the general picture was one of satisfaction. Similar studies have since been conducted by others, and the results tend to agree with Hoppock's. But interest in the topic persists.

IF YOU HAD IT TO DO AGAIN, WOULD YOU DO THE SAME THING?

Different ways of asking about job satisfaction can produce different results. While responses to the direct question about liking a job would imply that as many as nine out of ten workers are satisfied, responses to the less direct question—offering the possibility of reliving or reshaping careers—led to the conclusion that fewer people are happy in their work. Again, depending on which specific evidence a person chooses to accept, the incidence of job satisfaction drops roughly to two-thirds. Although this figure is somewhat lower than that derived from the answers to the first question, it is still clear that most workers report being contented in their jobs.

SATISFACTION INFERRED FROM JOB BEHAVIOR

While it is possible to learn about job satisfaction by asking workers how they feel about their jobs, there are other approaches. How a worker acts on his job can tell us something about his level of satisfaction. Some investigators have studied satisfaction by considering such aspects of work as worker turnover, absenteeism, firings, and other observable behavioral measures of job performance. The logic behind such an approach is that a person who is satisfied with his job will work well enough to keep his position, and it is likely that a person who is not satisfied with his job will perform in such a way as to effect his removal, voluntarily or involuntarily.

The evidence shows that a worker's behavior on the job is related to his level of satisfaction with the job. For example, Hulin (51, 52) found job satisfaction to be related to worker turnover, with satisfaction increasing and turnover decreasing in response to a program designed to achieve those goals. In a review of studies on job satisfaction and performance, Vroom (108) concluded that there is a consistent negative relationship between satisfaction and resigning (satisfied workers are less likely to resign than are dissatisfied workers) and a less consistent negative relationship between satisfaction and absences (dissatisfied workers are more likely to be absent). The relationship of job satisfaction to how well the person performs his job is another question: satisfaction has not generally been shown to be a factor in how well a person does his work.

Explanations of Satisfaction

As job satisfaction becomes a more important aspect of the study of human behavior, and as more is known about satisfaction itself, theories going beyond the answer to the simple question "Do you like your job?" have become necessary. Beyond stating that a person is satisfied doing what he likes to do, a number of more complex theoretical formulations have been offered. Two of the most important recent formulations have been the Two-Factor Theory of Frederick Herzberg and the Motivational Theory of Victor Vroom.

TWO-FACTOR THEORY

Reviewing the results of job satisfaction in a study involving over 28,000 workers, Herzberg and his associates at Pittsburgh (48) identified an apparent trend in the explanations of job satisfaction. They suggested that aspects of work reported as contributing to job satisfaction when favorable were not the things reported as sources of dissatisfaction when unfavorable. Correcting a source of dissatisfaction would therefore not necessarily produce satisfaction. In this formulation, there were different explanations for the two attitudes, satisfaction and dissatisfaction. One was not simply the lack of the other, in the way that health is the absence of sickness.

Herzberg and his associates concluded that factors which contributed primarily to satisfaction were *job content* factors: according to this theory, satisfaction is a function of what the person does on the job. Factors mentioned most often in regard to job dissatisfaction were defined as *job context* factors. These are fringe aspects of a job such as pay, social relationships, working conditions, and surroundings, matters not directly included in what the worker actually does. Rather, they are more relevant to the conditions of work.

The Herzberg formulation has stimulated many studies; however, most of these have not supported the two-factor theory. For example, in an investigation of 1,021 insurance agents, Ewen (29) found some context factors (Manager Interest, Training Policies, Salary) related to satisfaction and some content factors (Prestige or Recognition) related to dissatisfaction, contrary to predictions made from the two-factor theory. In spite of results like these, the Herzberg formulation has focused attention on a matter that needed more systematic research and has stimulated many studies, adding to our knowledge of occupational psychology.

MOTIVATIONAL THEORY

As do most approaches to job satisfaction, the two-factor theory places considerable emphasis on the conditions of work and on the work itself as the determinants of satisfaction. The work and its setting have been shown to be important factors. Because satisfaction is an individual matter, perhaps even more so than is success, it is also necessary to take into account individual personality factors, which play a major role in a person's attitudes.

In his discussion of work motivation, Vroom has conceptualized job satisfaction in terms of the attractiveness of a particular job for a person and his expectations about the rewards he will obtain from that job. Satisfaction is explained as a function of the relationship between the *work situation* and the *worker himself*. Using this approach, Vroom (107) investigated satisfaction, taking into account the extent to which a person reported participating in decisions in his job (a characteristic of the work) and his need for independence and degree of authoritarianism (characteristics of the worker). A person's satisfaction was found to be a function of both these types of variables. For instance, participation in decisions was most positively correlated with satisfaction among workers who had a high need for independence and a low degree of authoritarianism. This correlation was not as evident for workers with a low need for independence and a high degree of authoritarianism. The results of other studies are consistent with Vroom's explanation, and it is likely that his conceptualization will prove to be a useful and heuristic theoretical statement.

The Relationship between Aptitude and Satisfaction

What, then, do we conclude about the relationship between aptitude and satisfaction? It is obvious that no simple statement will be comprehensive enough to include all of the complexities of the relationship. There have been many studies of aptitude and many studies of job satisfaction. Surprisingly few studies, however, have looked at the relationship or the interaction of these two variables. Because of the nature of the variables, the effect of aptitude on satisfaction seems a more logical topic than does the effect of satisfaction on aptitude, although satisfaction may be expected to affect the direction and degree of use of aptitude.

Even without conclusive evidence about the nature of the relationship between these two variables, some conclusions can be drawn. First, there is some connection between the work setting and job satisfaction. There is a positive relationship between socioeconomic or prestige level of the job and level of satisfaction. Workers in higher-level jobs tend, on the average, to be happier with their work than are employees at the lower levels. Second, as seen in many studies, intelligence is related to job level. It might be concluded, from observing the relationship of aptitude to job level and that of job satisfaction to job level, that a relationship exists between aptitude and job satisfaction.

Job satisfaction is not simply a function of the level of the job or of the individual's level of aptitude. Instead, as with general satisfaction, it depends on the interaction between the demands of the position and the person's aptitudes. A person who possesses more aptitude than the job requires will tend to become dissatisfied and leave the job. For different reasons, a person with lower aptitude than most of his co-workers will tend to leave a position more quickly than a person who has the average amount of aptitude for the particular position. Individuals move in the direction of positions appropriate for their aptitudes, so that those who are unduly strained by the demands of their jobs and those who have aptitudes not challenged by their positions tend to move to other employment.

Aptitude plays a role in the level of occupation that a person selects and successfully pursues. Aptitude is important as a factor in satisfaction, in that the worker who has selected an occupation that allows him to make use of his abilities and to feel that he is adequately rewarded for his efforts is most likely to find satisfaction in his work.

Summary

This chapter has discussed aptitude as a psychological dimension in the division of labor. On measures of general intelligence, there is a definite hierarchy among occupations, but most occupations have distributions similar to an overall average. Within each occupation there is considerable variation, ranging from the very able to the less able. By the same token, there is considerable overlap among occupations on levels of intelligence. With the refinement of aptitude measurement, it has become possible to determine the distribution of specific aptitudes along occupational lines. Aptitudes are distributed in a manner similar to that of the distribution of general intelligence, with some aptitudes having special relevance for certain occupations.

The relationship between aptitude and success is not clear, partly because of difficulty in defining success. Success in an occupation, or how well a person is doing at the moment, is different from success in a career, or long-term handling of movement from position to position. Individuals tend to gravitate to jobs that demand their level of aptitude. Additional increments of aptitude, beyond meeting the necessary minimum required by a job, do not necessarily improve one's chances of success.

The relationship between aptitude and satisfaction has been the topic of a few investigations. Aptitude is indirectly related to satisfaction in that the more able workers tend to take higher-level positions, and these positions tend to be associated with greater satisfaction. More important than the absolute level of the job or the individual's aptitude is the relationship between these two factors. An individual is most satisfied with his job when the demands of the job are approximately at his level of aptitude and when he feels that the job offers him the opportunity for use and expression of his talents.

chapter five

Occupational
Personality
Patterns

In the preceding chapter, the psychological variable of aptitude was discussed in relation to the division of labor. Aptitude is clearly related to job level, with differences in aptitude occurring between occupations. The wide range of talents shown by the workers within a given occupational level, however, makes it obvious that aptitude is not the only determinant of job level. This chapter discusses other psychological variables that are relevant to the distribution of workers and to occupational choice.

Personality and Occupations

A man's personality gives us some basis for understanding the way he behaves; characteristic ways of behaving are one way of defining personality. We expect people with certain personality traits to act in certain ways. For example, if thinking about a friend has led us to the conclusion that he is a shy, quiet person, it would come as a surprise to see him arguing violently for a particular point of view in a large meeting. That kind of behavior just would not fit into our understanding of him.

In order to gain an understanding of behavior that goes beyond the simple description of events, however, it is necessary to have concepts that will bring together varying observations. Personality theorists have developed a number of such familiar constructs: needs, values, traits, and interests. Some aspects of personality are readily observable from behavior, and speculation about the nature of the concepts involved is at a minimum. For example, aptitude can be exhibited in a fairly direct way, in learning. In some ways, ability is the most easily observed and measured aspect of behavior, for it involves performing a task. Partly because it is, we know more about ability than about any other single aspect of personality.

Interests are almost as easily observed and measured as ability. Individuals differ in their preferences, and it is possible to categorize people on the basis of their likes and dislikes. Such preferences differ in intensity and importance within an individual. Some preferences are easily modified, while others can be changed, if at all, only as the result of tremendous effort. Likes and dislikes for occupations fit consistently into categories and are therefore extremely useful in the study of behavior. Almost as much is known about interests as is known about aptitudes.

Occupational Categorization

Among the methods of categorizing individuals, occupation is one of the most widely understood. While not everyone understands a description of a person as a "paranoid," characterization of a person as an office clerk does convey meaning to most people. The mention of an occupation usually evokes ideas of characteristics ("office clerks are neat and orderly"), and the evidence on occupational stereotypes shows that these stereotypes are stable and, to some degree, accurate.

It has even been suggested by a number of psychologists that the occupational classification of individuals probably has more stability and potential usefulness than does the conventional personality-classification approach. That is, instead of describing personality in terms of needs, drives, self-concepts, or other similar constructs, a more practical approach might be to begin the study of individuals in terms of occupational membership. This is the approach taken by some of the theorists who have emphasized the personality concept of interest, which, among personality characteristics, has been the one most successfully related to occupations.

Interests

With the exception of intelligence, more is known about interests than about any other single personality variable. Interests are activities and objects through which values are sought. In operational terms, interests are likes and dislikes for activities and objects.

If interests are likes and dislikes, vocational interests are likes and dislikes for things related to work. Early in the study of interests, it was thought that it did not really matter how an investigator ascertained a subject's interests. That is, interests were taken variously as what a person claimed to be interested in, how his likes and dislikes compared with those of other men, what kinds of activities he engaged in, or how much he knew about a topic. When the interest studies were compared and found to differ extensively in results and interpretations, it soon became evident that there was a need to refine the concept of interests.

Interpretations of Interests

The studies of vocational interests suggest that the findings from these studies can be separated into categories, depending on the type of interest data. Four interpretations of interests have been adopted: expressed, inventoried, manifest and tested.

Expressed interests are defined by statements a person makes about his interests. These statements are usually taken at face value, so that a person who says he wants to become an engineer is said to have an interest in engineering. Expressed interests were the first major definition of interests, with the others evolving later.

Inventoried interests are also expressions of likes and dislikes by an individual; however, many statements made by an individual are summed up and compared with statements made by others. Inventoried interests are not simply single statements; they are statistically treated statements, which yield scores. When psychologists speak of interests, in most cases they refer to inventoried interests, because most research has been conducted and the most useful knowledge has been produced about inventoried interests.

Manifest interests are defined in terms of the person's overt activities. An individual may say that he likes to participate in sports, but if he never goes out of his way to participate, then we conclude that he has expressed an interest in participating in sports, but that his manifest interests do not lie in that area. A boy who repairs automobiles as a hobby, taking things apart and putting them back together, would be said to manifest mechanical interests.

Tested interests are defined by what a person learns, on the theory that he learns about what interests him. These interests are inferred from the person's knowledge as measured by tests of information. It is not difficult to construct such tests, but they need constant updating as fields change. Although tested interests have shown good potential for usefulness, few tests of interests have developed. A person's interests, whether expressed, inventoried, manifest, or tested, usually show some consistency. When there is conflict between the results of one kind of interest measure and the results of another, the reason for the discrepancy is likely to tell something about the person tested that is useful in counseling and in decision making.

Measurement of Interests

Even when discussion of interests is limited to inventoried interests, there are differences in approaches to measurement; each approach involves assumptions about the nature of interests. Although the three different approaches have produced interest factors that are quite similar, the variations in assumptions are reflected in the three approaches to interest measurement: the empirical, the rational, and the factor analytic.

THE EMPIRICAL APPROACH

The empirical approach to interest measurement is best illustrated in the work of E. K. Strong, Jr. (88, 89), who devoted most of his career to the study of vocational interests. Strong began with the assumption that men who like and dislike the same things will choose the same kinds of activities. Specifically, men with similar likes and dislikes will choose the same or similar occupations. In order to substantiate this assumption, one would have to gather data about the likes and dislikes of men in selected occupations and compare their preferences with those of men in other occupations and with those of men in general. This is essentially what Strong did, validating his assumptions with empirical data.

Strong began his work on interests at the Carnegie Institute of Technology in Pittsburgh after World War I. He later moved to Stanford University and continued the development of his interest inventory. Various kinds of activities and preferences were included and tried in the inventory. After a suitable collection of items was established on one occupation, Strong proceeded to obtain data from additional occupational groups and to demonstrate that those groups too could be differentiated from men in general and from each other.

The evidence supported the assumption that men in different occupations have characteristically different likes and dislikes. From these beginning efforts to differentiate between a few specific occupations, Strong established a single reference group, called men in general, against which occupations could be compared. The scale for a specific occupation was determined by differences between the interests of the men in that occupational group and the interests of men in general.

This approach has been continued and elaborated on, making the Strong Vocational Interest Blank (SVIB) the best available validated interest inventory. For forty years this instrument has been the most widely studied measure of interests, and the recent revision of the SVIB promises to continue the tradition of usefulness. A sample SVIB profile, for an 18-year-old college freshman, is shown in Figure 5–1.

THE RATIONAL APPROACH

The rational approach to interest measurement begins with assumptions about the nature of interests and about the existence of certain kinds of interests. In empirical measurement, the first concern is how test items are related to criteria of performance, or what kinds of relationships are found in data. When successfully implemented, the rational approach has the advantage of assuring a meaningful theoretical interpretation of whatever findings arise from data. G. F. Kuder hypothesized the existence of interest factors and then constructed an inventory to measure these presumed factors.

Like Strong, Kuder began with a list of activities and preferences that were logically related to the interest factors. Individuals responded to this inventory, and, using statistical techniques that stressed internal-consistency analysis, Kuder purified and refined the scales. The result was an inventory based on a theoretical formulation of the structure of interests, with scales constructed to measure the interest factors. This measure, the Kuder Vocational Preference Record Form C, has been widely used and has proved helpful in understanding interests. In recent years it has been supplemented by relating the scores on this measure to actual occupations.

Three subsequent Kuder instruments have thus been developed, building in part on work from the Form C. The Kuder Form D, Occupational, employed the same items and introduced an empirically oriented scoring system similar to Strong's: individual responses were compared with those from occupational groups, and a person's score reflected the similarity between his answers and the answers of men in a particular occupational group. A later form of this inventory is the Kuder Occupational Interest Survey Form DD, which introduces a

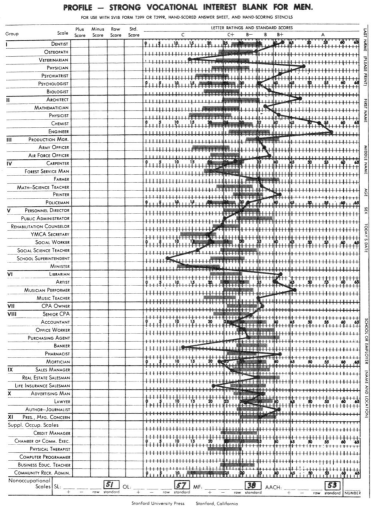

FIGURE 5-1. *SVIB profile for 18-year-old male college freshman. Reprinted with permission of the publisher from the* Manual for Strong Vocational Interest Blanks for Men and Women *by Edward K. Strong, Jr., revised by David P. Campbell (Stanford: Stanford University Press, 1966), p. 14.*

complicated new method of scoring, eliminating the men in general group. The Kuder General Interest Survey Form E is scored for 10 types of interests, as shown in Figure 5–2. The effectiveness of these newer instruments will be determined by their relationship to actual choices of occupations and to performance of men in their occupations.

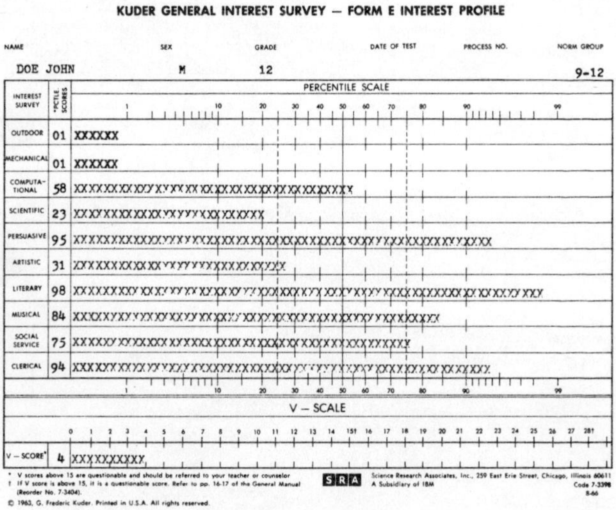

FIGURE 5–2. *Kuder General Interest Survey— Form E Interest Profile. Copyright 1963, G. Frederic Kuder. Reproduced by permission of the publisher, Science Research Associates, Inc.*

THE FACTOR ANALYTIC APPROACH

This approach to interest measurement is based on the assumption that the structure of interests can be best determined by the relationships found in various measures of interests. Although Strong factor analyzed the results of his empirically derived scales, and Kuder used a method resembling factor analysis in the refinement of his theoretically originated interest categories, the most complete factor analytic approach was taken by J. P. Guilford and associates (44).

Believing that previous measures had not taken motivation adequately into account, Guilford hypothesized or predicted the important interest factors, including motivation. His hypotheses were converted into operational terms, for which interest tests were constructed and given to Air Force enlisted men and officers. Scores were obtained and factor analyzed to produce the simplest, most psychologically meaningful structure of interests. As mentioned in the beginning chapter, the interest factors produced in this way were similar to those from the work of Strong and Kuder, suggesting that interests can be organized into general factors.

Interests and Occupations

Whatever the theoretical assumptions underlying an approach to interests, and whatever the method of measurement employed to determine a person's interests, the real proof of the importance of interests is their relationship to actual behavior. People are involved with occupations in a number of ways in the progress of a career, as will be discussed at some length in the chapter on careers. Questions to be asked about interests and different aspects of a person's occupational behavior include: Are interests related to the occupation a person enters? Can we predict a person's occupational membership from his interest scores? Can we predict the stability of a person's occupational membership from his interest scores?

INTERESTS AND OCCUPATIONAL MEMBERSHIP

The relationship between a man's interests and his occupational membership, of course, was basic to Strong's work. Positing that men in the same occupations would have similar likes and dislikes, Strong developed occupational interest scales that empirically differentiated one occupational group from other occupational groups and from a composite group of men in general. Strong constructed his occupational scales so that approximately 69 percent of each original criterion group would score A (high) on its own scale, 29 percent B+ and B, and approximately 2 percent C (low). When this kind of distribution is set up, then, and is found in later samples of the same population, as proved to be the case with Strong's inventory, it is clear that the resulting occupational-interest scores are related to occupational membership.

In developing the occupational scales, Strong found that occupations were clustered according to greater or lesser similarity of interests. Three similar lists of interest factors were presented earlier in this book; Strong's group factors were based on the intercorrelations of the specific occupational scales and on their logical similarity. At times the empirical relationship (the correlation) was paramount, producing some groups with strange combinations: the original Biological Sciences group, for example, included Artist and Architect. In the main, however, the groups made logical as well as statistical sense. With the revision of the Strong scale and the further development of new occupational groups, such as Computer Programmer and Rehabilitation Counselor, the groups have increased in number, coverage, and logical purity. The current groups on the Strong inventory were developed on the basis of the mean scores of the occupations on the scales, the intercorrelations between the scales, the similarity of occupational requirements for the occupations, and the history of previous interest-inventory research. Groups on the Strong inventory, then, are composed of occupations similar in interests, and because no other occupations have been found similar to CPA Owners or Presidents of Manufacturing Concerns, these occupations stand alone. The present list of groups (18) is as follows:

I. Biological Science	VII. CPA Owner
II. Physical Science	VIII. Business and Account-
III. Technical Supervision	ing
IV. Technical and Skilled	IX. Sales
Trades	X. Verbal-Linguistic
V. Social Service	XI. President, Manufac-
VI. Aesthetic-Cultural	turing Concern

In order to differentiate one occupational group from the others, it was necessary to establish an appropriate reference, or men in general, group. After trying a number of such reference groups, Strong ultimately developed a group that represented a sampling of the upper-level occupations, and with this group, he was able to differentiate the various higher-level occupations. Results with lower-level occupations, however, were not so positive. For a time it was thought that individuals in occupations that typically do not require college training, such as tabulating-machine operators or electricians, might lack differentiating interests, and it was not until Clark (21) developed a more appropriate men in general group, composed of tradesmen in general, that the vocational interests of skilled workers were satisfactorily identified. Semi-skilled workers still have not been adequately studied.

Differentiation of occupations according to the interests of the workers in them depends to a large extent on selecting a relevant reference group. Carrying this process one step further, it should be possible to differentiate *within* a large, heterogeneous occupational group, to differentiate between specialties within a given major occupation. Research with psychologists, engineers, and physicians has shown that it is possible. Psychologists are more similar to other psychologists than they are to men in general. By the process of comparison with psychologists in general, it is also possible to differentiate among specialists such as clinical, experimental, and social psychologists.

INTERESTS AND THE PREDICTION OF OCCUPATIONAL MEMBERSHIP

The prediction of people's occupational membership from their interests requires relating the interests measured before entry into the labor market to the eventual occupations entered. Employing such a procedure, Strong obtained interest measurements on a group of men while they were still in college. In one study 10 years later and in another 18 years later, these men were asked about their occupations and how they felt about their progress. The major data come from the 18-year follow-up study by Strong (89) of 663 men.

Summarizing the results of that study, interests shown during college were related to later occupational behavior. The highest average scores an individual received were on the scale for the occupation he actually engaged in. The chances were roughly 3 to 1 that a person would enter an occupation for which he had received an A on the scale. For low scores, the odds were even more supportive of the capacity of interests to predict later occupational membership. The chances were 5 to 1 against a person's entering an occupation if he had received a low score on that occupational scale. When the interest patterns of the men were analyzed by experts who judged the appropriateness of interest profiles for the occupations the men had entered, approximately two thirds of the men had interests judged to be compatible with their occupations.

INTERESTS AND THE PREDICTION OF STABILITY OF OCCUPATIONAL MEMBERSHIP

By using the 18-year follow-up, Strong had related the interests at college age to the occupation engaged in at the time of the follow-up, regardless of the changes and movements that might have occurred or that might occur in the future. This kind of data did not seek to answer the question of stability in an occupation. Earlier studies, however, were aimed directly at the topic of stability.

Occupational stability, like occupational membership, was found to be related to vocational interest scores (89). In a comparison of the interests of men who had made major occupational changes with those of men who had not made such changes, the following findings are relevant. Men remaining in an occupation had higher scores on the scale for that occupation than on other occupational scales. Also, men in a given occupation scored higher on the scale for that occupation than did men in other occupations or than did men who had entered that occupation and later left it. In addition, men who changed to a given occupation had lower scores on that occupational scale than did men who went directly from college into that occupation. A person's interests may be like those of people in his occupation before entering it (anticipatory socialization) or after entry (adaptation). But, as we have seen, interests tend to exist before training and are not significantly affected by adult experience.

Interests and Success

If a person likes his job, does he perform more successfully in it? Remembering the complex nature of success, we will look at some evidence on interests and success. Common sense would lead one to expect a meaningful relationship between interest in certain occupations and success achieved in them, but such a relationship does not always exist. Among the things to be considered in the study of interest and success are both success in the pre-vocational or training phase of the occupation and success in actually performing the job.

SUCCESS IN TRAINING

A common explanation students give for poor achievement in courses is that they just were not interested. If only they had been interested, then they would not have minded doing the work, and they would have done much better. If this kind of reasoning is valid, interests should be highly and positively correlated with measures of performance in courses and in training programs. Assuming the necessary minimum of aptitude for the topic, interest should be accompanied by good grades.

There have been numerous studies on the question of interest and grades, and the results have *not* supported the hypothesis that interests are an important factor in school or college achievement. How well a person does in his school work is more dependent on his ability, previous preparation, and desire to succeed in school than on whether or not he likes the material. As Strong (88) concluded, interests play a role in the kinds of courses a person chooses; when the person chooses a course and then finds that he does not like it, his interests may lead him not to choose other courses that are similar, but his achievement in the course will be a function primarily of variables other than interest. Completion of training is a different kind of success in training. As interests are important in selecting and remaining in an occupation, they might be expected to predict choice of courses and, consequently, continuation in a field of study. Strong (88) found that interest in dentistry was associated with likelihood of finishing dental training. Specifically, of students making A's on the Dentist scale, almost all completed dental school in 4–6 years; of those making C's on the scale, only 25% successfully completed the program. Completion of training is one kind of success that is clearly related to interests.

SUCCESS ON THE JOB

Since interests are related to the occupation a person chooses, it might follow that interests are important in how well he does the job he has chosen. Although this conclusion seems logical, there is little evidence to support it. Attempts to relate interests to success on the job have not been successful. Interests can assist in predicting the *direction* in which a person may go occupationally (the occupation he chooses), but they do not tell us much about his probable *level of achievement* in that occupation.

There is at least one important occupational exception to this conclusion: sales. In studies of salesmen in a number of fields, but particularly insurance, it has been established that the higher a person's interest scores in the area of sales, the greater the likelihood that the person will make a successful sales record. Why interests should be related to sales work is not clear, especially when attempts to relate success and interest in other types of occupations have generally been inconclusive. It has been suggested that selling is an occupation in which a person must find the activities personally congenial in order to perform them well. A salesman's success is directly dependent on how well he carries out his function, so that other things being equal, the greater the interest and the more congenial the work, the greater the likelihood that he will succeed (95).

Interests and Satisfaction

Satisfaction is the most logical and perhaps the most relevant aspect of a person's work adjustment of those that might be expected to relate to vocational interests. Interests are a person's likes and dislikes, and his satisfaction should be a function of his likes and their relevance to his job. If interests tell us anything about an individual's work life, they should tell us something about his work satisfaction.

SATISFACTION IN TRAINING

Unlike success, satisfaction does seem to be clearly related to interests. Although there have been few studies directly investigating this relationship, the evidence available does support it. Berdie (9), for example, found that engineering students who had engineering interest patterns were more satisfied with their curriculum than were engineering students who did not have this kind of pattern. Similarly, in other studies, students who have chosen college settings in which the dominant interest patterns are similar to their own are more satisfied with their college environment than students who have not chosen such an environment.

More persuasive than such studies of curriculum satisfaction and interests, however, are the data already reported on interests and the completion of training. Often a person will complete a single course even though he does not care for it and even though he is not satisfied with it. Completion of a training program, however, is a different story: persistence implies satisfaction of an interest. Because interests are related to the criterion of completing a training program, we conclude that having related interests is important for satisfaction in training.

SATISFACTION ON THE JOB

As it is the satisfied who stay with their jobs, the research on interests and stability in occupations suggests that workers who have vocational interests appropriate for their occupations tend to remain in those occupations and are the most satisfied with them. The conclusion follows almost too easily.

Among workers who stay on the job, are there differences in satisfaction levels? If there are differences, are they at all related to the interests of the workers? A number of studies conclude that among workers who stay with their jobs, the most satisfied are those whose interests are most similar to those of the men in that line of work. For example, Schwebel (80) found that interested pharmacists were more satisfied with their occupation than were pharmacists whose interest patterns were not appropriate to their occupation. Similarly, among policemen and among clerical workers, Kates (54, 55) found interests to be related to overall job satisfaction. Interests, then, are useful in understanding satisfaction, both in the behavioral sense of staying on the job and in the attitudinal sense of liking the job.

Values

Another approach to the study of personality and its relevance to a man's occupation is through values. Values, it will be recalled, were defined as objectives that one seeks to attain. Values are ends desired for the well-being of the organism, the satisfactions achieved when needs and drives are met. A man's values should thus tell us something about his occupational behavior.

Value as a Personality Construct

Like interests, values have been emphasized by students of personality who wanted to characterize the positive aspects of normal human adjustment. Thus, values do not rely primarily on consideration of sickness or pathology for their grounding.

The primary theoretical impetus for treating values as a dimension of personality came from the philosopher Eduard Spranger, who stressed the positive side of human nature. Believing that men are best understood in terms of their motivations and aims, Spranger posited six types of men: Theoretical, Economic, Aesthetic, Social, Political, and Religious. This conceptualization of values in personality was adopted by Allport and Vernon (1) and operationalized in their development of *The Study of Values: A Scale for Measuring the Dominant Interests in Personality*. The similarity of values to interests is indicated by the title of the inventory. With this instrument it was possible to measure the relative strengths of these values within a person: scores obtained by this method are termed *ipsative*. In these inventories, the choice of an item that raises the score of one value must at the same time decrease the score on another value. Normative scores, or scores that can be expected from groups, were developed later, permitting the comparison of values of different individuals.

Values in Vocational Development

Among the first to incorporate values into a theory of vocational development were Eli Ginzberg and a group of associates, who presented their theory in their book, *Occupational Choice* (40). Ginzberg established three categories of sources of satisfaction from work. *Intrinsic* values are satisfactions derived from the activity itself: thus a musician who finds satisfaction in making music finds intrinsic value in his occupation. *Extrinsic* values are the returns that a job provides: the best known extrinsic value of a job is probably money. *Concomitant* values are those aspects of work that are part of the job situation, although not necessarily part of the work itself: for example, in many jobs the appeal lies not in what one does, but in the interaction with others a person enjoys while doing his work.

A somewhat different approach to the study of values in occupational behavior was that of Richard Centers (20), discussed earlier in this book. Centers provided a list of jobs described in terms of values that would be met in them. For example, one job was described as being "A job where you could express your feelings, ideas, talent, or skill." Workers at different socioeconomic levels selected different values, the clearest finding being that workers at the lower levels valued security the most, while men at the upper levels considered self-expression and interesting experiences to be the most important values. These results are consistent with the idea that more basic aspects of adjustment (needs and values), in this case security, must be achieved before secondary and perhaps derivative aspects such as opportunity for self-expression can be valued.

Recognizing the variety of values relevant to occupational behavior, Super (94) developed the Work Values Inventory to measure the strength of values with specific reference to work. Various forms of the WVI have provided both ipsative measures of values (relative strengths within a person) and normative value measures (strength of a value in a person compared to its strength in a normative sample population). The grouping of the values was accomplished according to their intrinsic, extrinsic, and concomitant qualities; such grouping has had some empirical support in recent research.

To determine how these work values relate to life values, psychologists have studied general life values and specific work values together. Relating scores on the Allport-Vernon-Lindzey *Study of Values* scales (2) with scores on work-values factors, Kinnane and Gaubinger (57) found the values to be related in the expected way. For example, the AVL theoretical value related significantly to the heuristic-creative factor in work values. The authors concluded that the AVL reflects abstract values, while the WVI, as intended, measures values in a work setting, in which the value judgments have clear practical implications.

Values in Occupations

If values play an important role in an individual's vocational development, the occupation chosen or entered should to some extent reflect his value structure. There is good evidence that values are important in vocational decisions such as the choice of pre-occupational program or of major in college. That is, the values ranked highest differ from one program to the next, and the values ranked highest by students in a major such as engineering are typically appropriate for that group.

As is the case with some other psychological variables, the groups most often studied are college students at various levels of training. In the case of values, this emphasis has been especially noticeable, since the older instruments developed to measure values were designed for college use. *Theoretical* values are frequently reported as high in students of education, engineering, medicine, natural science, and social studies (46, 78, 87), while business students tend to have high *economic* values (82, 87, 105). *Artistic* values are seen in majors that emphasize expression, such as drama and literature, while *religious* values, quite appropriately, are found to be high in seminaries.

In a study of the reasons given by over 4500 college students for selecting their educational objectives (76), the basic values expressed were: (1) working with others in a helping manner; (2) earning large amounts of money, social status, and prestige; and (3) having the opportunity to be creative and to use special talents. The students in the various college majors, for the most part, valued those things relevant to their course of study. For example, students valuing highly the chance to have a great deal of money, social status, and prestige tended to be in commercially oriented programs. Students valuing the opportunity for service tended to be in programs emphasizing service (e.g., social work, pre-medicine, education), and students not valuing service highly were in other kinds of programs (e.g., engineering, natural science, agriculture).

Of more direct relevance to occupational behavior are the work values of men actually employed. Using a sample including psychiatrists, psychologists, teachers, priests, lawyers, CPAs, and engineers, Normile (69) compared the work-value scores of these groups. There were significant differences among the seven occupational groups. Priests were the highest on altruism and the lowest on economic returns; such scores are consistent with some expectations of men in the priesthood. The psychiatrists, lawyers, and engineers placed higher value on intellectual stimulation than did the teachers, while the teachers valued security more highly than did the psychiatrists or psychologists. In other research, Peace Corps teacher trainees were found to have high scores on altruism, aesthetics, creativity, intellectual stimulation, variety, and way of life and to have low scores on economic returns, security, surroundings, and associates. With the possible exception of way of life, these values are presented as the anticipated profile for people motivated to enter "helping" occupations of a novel type.

The number and the consistency of different studies relating values to pre-occupational and occupational behavior and to other variables known to be important in this area of a man's life effect acceptance of the importance of values in occupational behavior. Though not as completely researched or validated as are interests, the concept of values has a place in occupational psychology. Values, like interests, appear before occupational experience and seem to affect attitudes and behavior.

Needs

Unlike interests, which have been investigated largely by vocational psychologists, needs have been studied primarily by psychologists concerned with the structure and functioning of personality, particularly in abnormal and disturbed individuals. As a concept, however, needs have been important in the theoretical formulations of a number of writers on vocational psychology. Some researchers studying occupations and their role in personality adjustment have found the concept of need useful.

Needs in Theories of Vocational Development

Anne Roe, as mentioned in Chapter 2, was among the first to use needs explicitly and extensively in a theory of vocational development, taking Maslow's system as her frame of reference.

One of Roe's first research interests was the effect of alcohol on creativity, particularly in artists (she found that alcohol does not make artists more creative). Later, following an interest in the development of eminent scientists, Roe sought to find out what aspects of personality differentiated scientists in various fields. From her data, which included material from standardized tests, projective tests, and interviews, Roe concluded that differences in early childhood experiences were reflected in later choices of occupation. More specifically, she found that men from homes oriented to the needs of children, homes that put a premium on warm, satisfactory relationships within the family, tended to enter occupations that provided further such warmth and support. Men whose occupations involved a minimum of contact with others on the job and for whom work was often a solitary activity characteristically came from homes in which the early relationships had not been close or rewarding.

Expanding the scope of her studies, Roe developed a theory of vocational choice based primarily on early childhood experiences in the home. The basic consideration in the theoretical model was atmosphere in the home, which was described as warm or cold. Attitudes toward the child followed from the home atmosphere and led to the different categories of parent-child relations.

These different types of parent-child relations were seen as producing a major orientation either *toward* persons or *not toward* persons. For example, the social scientists' characteristic orientation was toward persons, and the physical scientists' orientation was not toward persons, but toward objects or ideas. According to the theory, it is these orientations that lead to interest development and occupational choice. Roe further formalized her theory in a classification of all occupations on the two dimensions of field and level. The field (group) dimension of this system is based on interests, on the primary focus of the occupation, and the level dimension is defined in terms of responsibility, capacity, and skill in the occupation (74).

Edward Bordin and associates (14) at the University of Michigan developed a different approach to needs in vocational development, similar to Murray's system in its psychoanalytic origins. This approach begins with the assumption that development in an individual is continuous, so that infantile experience is related to behavior as an adult. It is also assumed that the complex activities of an adult provide the same sources of gratification as the simple activities of a child. Finally, Bordin theorizes, like Freud, that the strengths and constellations of a person's needs are fairly well established early in life, perhaps by the time the individual is six years old. Occupations are classified in terms of their different potentials for need gratification. An individual's needs, then, can be expected to offer an understanding of his choice of occupation and of the kinds of satisfactions he enjoys as a result of his choice.

Needs and Occupations

It is one thing to hypothesize relationships between needs and occupations, according to a logical schema and explanation. It is something else to obtain evidence in support of these basic hypotheses. While some formulations about needs and personality make good sense and have a certain amount of appeal, in general the data have not lived up to the expectations. No generalizations can be made; however, there is evidence for some relationships, which are considered below.

The theory proposed by Roe inspired a series of investigations to test hypotheses derived from her theory. In the main, the results of these investigations did not support the expected relationships between parent-child relations and occupational choice, although there were some isolated positive findings. In a major study, *The Origin of Interests*, Roe and Siegelman (75) analyzed the parent-child relations of college students, male and female engineers, and male and female social workers. They concluded that early social experience may be related to later personal orientation (toward persons or not toward persons), but that explanations of vocational choice must take into account many things in addition to early parent-child relationships.

The relationship of needs and need satisfactions to job satisfaction was the topic of an earlier monograph by R. H. Schaffer (79). From each person studied, Schaffer obtained measures of the strength of needs and also of the extent to which these needs were met in the person's job. In his sample of men in higher-level occupations, the strongest needs were creativity and challenge, as well as mastery, achievement, and social welfare. There were significant relationships between satisfaction of the three strongest needs and overall job satisfaction; such relationships demonstrate the importance of personal needs in job satisfaction.

In a study involving measures of needs and indications of needs met by specific jobs, Walsh (109) found that people emphasize those aspects of a job that meet their own needs. Thus, the same need can be met in a number of different occupations, depending on how the individual worker structures his job. By the same token, a variety of needs can be met by the same occupation, again depending on the worker's approach to his job. This variation in emphasis in part explains the failure of research to relate specific needs to specific jobs. Perhaps a more crucial issue than what particular needs are met by specific jobs is the *role* that the worker selects for himself within the context of the job. Evidence on needs and occupations also comes from investigators using the Bordin approach, who have studied the personality characteristics and the need gratifications of different occupational groups. In a comparison of prospective lawyers, social workers, and dentists, Nachmann (67) found differences in the backgrounds and family situations from which people in these three occupational groups came. The law students came from homes in which aggressive impulses (needs) were accepted and thus developed, fathers were dominant and masculine, and discipline was achieved through verbal control and fairness, which reinforced needs for verbal control. The dental students' homes, on the other hand, did not accept aggressive impulses. In those homes also, the father was dominant, but here the discipline was masculine or actively aggressive, and curiosity and aggressive needs were turned inward. The social workers came from homes in which the fathers were ineffective and the mothers were the source of strength and emotional support, leading these men to be concerned for the welfare of others and to be verbally rather than physically controlling. Such findings illustrate the role of psychological needs such as aggression, curiosity, and compassion in occupational choice and performance.

Traits

Traits are consistencies in a person's behavior. In a sense, then, the personality dimensions already mentioned can be considered traits. Interests are reflected in a consistency in likes and dislikes of certain activities or materials. Values are goals or ends that a person believes to be desirable. Needs are seen in a person's drive for specific objects. Rather than any one of these constructs, traits represent a more general kind of consistency in behavior. That is, they more nearly represent the *style* of behavior rather than the *content* of the behavior itself. Traits are less a matter of *what* is done than of the *way* in which it is done.

Trait as a Personality Construct

As a central construct in personality theory, traits have been well emphasized in the writings of Gordon Allport. Stressing the consistency or unity of the personality and focusing on the study of the individual rather than groups, Allport felt that *true traits* are seen only within individuals. *Common traits* are the similarities observed in different people. In his studies of expressive behavior, Allport attempted to document consistency in the way a person acts, as seen in his style and mannerisms.

Another psychologist who has made much use of traits is Raymond Cattell. Relying on factor analysis, which clusters items together according to their relationships, Cattell proposed two major types of traits: surface traits and source traits. The *surface traits* are those clusters of behavior or variables that seem to go together; *source traits* are the underlying variables that actually determine the behavior engaged in. The development of measures of surface traits was based on information taken largely from three sources: life records, self ratings, and objective tests. Relying mainly on the factor analysis of life records, or behavior in everyday situations, Cattell has identified presumed underlying source traits. He considers these traits to be the type of variable that is potentially most useful in the study of personality. Although produced differently, the general structure of Cattell's trait theory is similar to that of Allport.

Traits as consistencies in behavior were, in most cases, inferred from personal observations and evaluations of experience. Tests or test items were constructed to measure these suggested traits. The traits were then factor analyzed or otherwise purified. In the literature about personality traits and occupations, this approach was referred to as the "trait-and-factor" method; the term recognizes both the trait concept and the further work of factor analysis.

Traits in Theories of Vocational Development

Trait-and-factor approaches to the study of personality appeared early in the history of applied psychology. By World War I, significant advances had been made in the measurement of intelligence and in successfully relating it to occupational membership. After the war, as further progress was made in measurement and psychological testing, specific aptitudes were identified and measured. Specific-aptitude tests were followed by the development of personality inventories and later by interest inventories.

The trait-and-factor approach to relating personality to occupations was largely the result of two elements. First, there was progress in the identification and measurement of personal characteristics. With improved measures of aptitudes, traits, interests, and other personality dimensions, differential psychology permitted the more exact description of personal characteristics. Second, the value of using occupations as a classification system was recognized. It became evident that groups of persons in similar occupations did have some similar characteristics and that there was some stability to these characteristics. Whereas Strong studied occupational groups in terms of their interests, and Roe theorized about occupational membership as partly a function of needs that influenced the choice of occupation, an example of a current approach that makes direct use of personality type and occupational membership is that of Holland (49).

Reasoning that most people can be classified according to six major orientations to life, Holland proposed that individuals select occupations and job environments that will suit their personality types. He developed a classification system that dealt with both personality and occupations.

Holland's six personality types, or major orientations, are:

1. Realistic

2. Intellectual

3. Social

4. Conventional

5. Enterprising

6. Artistic

The meanings of these categories are partially indicated by the titles. The *Realistic* type is the individual who is active and aggressive, and who prefers concrete things to the abstract. This type of person is most often found in occupations such as those of engineer or forester and in the trades and industry. The *Intellectual* type is task-oriented and somewhat asocial; he prefers to think things out rather than to act on them; he has a need to understand. Intellectual types are characteristically found in occupations such as those of biologist, chemist, independent research worker, and zoologist. The *Social* type is gregarious and relates to others through his feelings. Often he is in a helping occupation such as clinical psychologist, teacher of exceptional children, or social worker. The *Conventional* type prefers a good deal of structure in his work activities and chooses jobs such as those of bank examiner, court stenographer, or statistician. The *Enterprising* type enjoys selling and ambiguous activities that allow him to compete with others. This type is most frequently employed in occupations such as hotel manager, real estate salesman, and television producer. The *Artistic* type is concerned with expression of feelings and, when possible, is employed in the artistic occupations.

Using the concept of these personality types, Holland has been able to relate personality characteristics to important occupational behaviors such as vocational interests, post–high school plans, and vocational preferences. Most of the evidence supporting his formulation has come from studies of students not yet in the labor force, however, and how well the types describe workers has yet to be established.

Traits in Occupations

The discussion of personality variables such as interests, values, and needs has shown that there are relationships between these variables and occupations. That is, individuals with certain kinds of interests, values, and needs are more likely to choose one kind of job than another. These relationships reflect consistencies in behavior and suggest the theoretical validity of the personality constructs themselves, as well as of their relevance to occupational classification.

In addition to studies that show relationships between interests, values, and needs on the one hand and occupations on the other, some studies of occupational groups are done with psychological inventories of personality traits that reflect behavior style. For example, occupations have been studied by means of the Minnesota Multiphasic Personality Inventory (MMPI), a test originally designed to discriminate between groups of psychiatric patients. Recently the MMPI's diagnostic scales have been shown to measure modes of behavior characteristic of normals, as well as the behavior of neurotics and psychotics. On the MMPI, differences between certain occupational groups have been found, such as in a comparison of advertising men and engineers. The two groups had similar profiles, reflecting tendencies to put themselves in the best possible light and to be self-confident, energetic, and sociable. The advertising men, as could be expected, had scores that differed from the average more than did the scores of the engineers. The difference was especially marked on a scale believed related to uncommon freedom of expression and strong esthetic interests (102).

There have also been a few studies of occupations with other trait measures, such as the California Psychological Inventory (CPI), a test somewhat like the MMPI but more appropriate for normal populations. This test has been used in extensive studies of personality involving Air Force officers, as well as in studies of students in engineering, medicine, and physical science. Results on these tests and others have shown that some occupations do have scores that differ from the average, but it is difficult to interpret the meaning of these scores. The occupational differences are less striking than the amount of overlapping between the occupations.

The early trait-and-factor approach to personality and occupations was primarily concerned with finding how selected occupational groups (or student groups preparing for occupations) would score on personality tests. The profiles for various occupations on these tests were then known, but it was almost impossible to use the available knowledge in a more general theory of occupations based on traits. As more inclusive and sophisticated theories of vocational development have become available, descriptions of occupational personality characteristics have taken on more meaning. For example, Roe explains vocational choice as a function of needs and early childhood experience, and Holland discusses vocational behavior, settings, and personality types. Such theories offer the possibility of better understanding of personality traits and occupations.

It has been recognized for some time that an occupation can accommodate a wide variety of personality types, and that any one person can fit into a wide variety of jobs. There is evidence of relationships between some traits and some occupations (e.g., salesmen are indeed usually somewhat more aggressive than the general population), but it is now known that matching men and jobs is not a simple, direct process. Within many occupations, there is some latitude as to *which* specific role a person may play. There is even more latitude in *how* a person plays the role he selects. For example, lawyers are similar in many ways, but also there are many types of lawyers, and there are even varied ways of being the same kind of lawyer. A lawyer may enjoy working with clients, or he may prefer to do research by himself; he can be interested in making public presentations, or he can limit his expression to writing. His *style*, or the way in which he handles his obligations, is, in part, a function of his traits. The next advances in trait-and-factor occupational psychology may well be in the understanding of personality as *style* in an occupation.

Self-Concept

The final aspect of personality that has been studied in relation to occupational behavior is that of the self-concept. It has been found that people describe themselves in terms of interests, values, needs, and styles of behavior, and some psychologists have stressed the importance of the individual's own image of himself as a significant determinant of behavior.

Self-Concept as a Personality Construct

The idea of *self* as a primary personality construct dates back almost to the beginning of American psychology. William James (53) wrote of the self, or the "empirical me," as everything a person would call his own, meaning his physical being, his relationships with others, and his activities (45). Following James, the definitions and explanations of self have been many and varied.

George Herbert Mead (63) introduced a concept of self that was important in its effects on personality study. For Mead, the self was the result of experience with others: a person learns to think of himself as others think of him. Thus, the self is a socially formed phenomenon, and because of dependence on others, the person learns to have a number of different selves for different groups of others. Thus, a person may act one way with his parents and another way with his classmates.

A *self-concept* has usually been considered to be the picture a person has of himself. This specific term is partly an outgrowth of phenomenological psychology, which states that a person reacts to reality as he sees it. That is, all that a person experiences goes through his own interpretation system. Especially in regard to his own personality, an individual organizes, interprets, and understands what he knows of himself in terms that are acceptable to him. Of course, it is generally accepted that one's personality is more complex than merely those aspects that are known to oneself. In the study of self-concepts, "phenomenal" aspects are those attributes of which the individual is aware, while the "nonphenomenal" aspects are the feelings, motivations, knowledge, and perceptions that are unconscious, or not evident to the person (112). The phenomenal or conscious self-concept has been of more interest to those concerned with studying personality and occupations than has the nonphenomenal.

Self-Concept in Theories of Vocational Development

Among the first writers to discuss the self-concept in relation to vocational behavior was Carter (19), who described self-concept as the product of a person's attempts to make a successful adjustment to his environment. Within the limits presented by the environment and by the basic genetic endowment of the individual, a person identifies with people in a particular occupation. If this identification is a practical one—that is, one for which he has the necessary interests and aptitudes and which provides satisfactory rewards—it continues and exerts an integrating influence on the personality by strengthening a particular concept of the self.

Specifically in relation to vocational interests, Bordin (13) postulated that, in answering an interest inventory, a person indicates his acceptance of a concept of himself in terms of occupational stereotypes. The self-concept is thus translated directly into feelings and behaviors related to occupations.

Self-concept theory has been one of the main bases for Super's theory of vocational development (92). He regards vocational development as a lifelong process and describes self-concepts and their role in a career in successive periods of life. This formulation will be discussed in detail in a later chapter, when self-concepts are considered from a different perspective.

Self-Concepts and Occupations

Like the other aspects of personality, self-concepts should have some theoretical and empirical relationship to occupations in order to be useful in occupational psychology. How do one's self-concepts relate to the occupations he prefers, to the training he undertakes, and to his feeling about the job he enters?

As a person considers the kind of individual he is, and as he considers the types of people in different jobs, he comes to the conclusion that he is more like some workers than like others, that some persons in some occupations have characteristics similar to his own. Also, students come to see themselves as similar to men in occupations to which they aspire. For example, self-descriptions and ideal self-concepts of high school boys are more similar to the stereotypes of occupations they prefer than to those of the occupations they do not prefer (11). Other studies have found that students' self-concepts are consistent with their concepts of men in the occupations they prefer (65, 70).

Some occupations have long, rigid training programs, which necessitate early decision, while other jobs have relatively short, uncomplicated requirements and may be decided upon early or late. In general, the higher-level occupations have the more involved and more demanding training requirements. Medicine is a good example of an occupation that demands an early declaration. It has been suggested that an early choice of medicine as a career reflects a crystallized or stabilized self-concept. The rule of early commitment necessarily preceding extensive training, however, is not without exception: law, for example, is a profession that can be chosen at the end of college or later. Law schools permit a variety of undergraduate majors, but law training itself is extensive and prolonged.

In a study of applicants to medical school, Stephenson (84) found that of those denied entry on their first application, 30 percent eventually were admitted to a medical school and another 32 percent ended up in some job related to medicine. These men, even before medical school, evidently thought of themselves as members of the medical profession and made great efforts to turn that self-concept into reality.

After entry into a job, how well a person feels that his self-concept fits in with what is expected of him is an important factor in his feelings about his job. The discrepancies between self-concepts and occupational role requirements, between ideal occupational concepts and required occupational role, and between actual self-concepts and ideal role concepts are *inversely* related to job satisfaction (16). That is, the greater the difference between self image and job image, the less the satisfaction the person experiences on the job.

A person's self-concept, his picture of himself, influences his actions and helps determine the occupations he prefers, the kind of training he undertakes, and the degree of satisfaction he experiences on his job.

Summary

The topic of this chapter has been occupational personality patterns, or the relationships between personality variables and occupations. Interests, values, needs, traits, and self-concepts can each be considered as personality constructs, as elements in theories of vocational development, and as concepts with relationships to occupation.

Of the variables discussed, interest has been the most useful to occupational psychology. Men in different occupations tend to have different likes and dislikes. Among students, interests are clearly related to later occupational choices and to stability within later occupations. Values, both work values and general life values, are related to occupational behavior. Values operate in ways that are similar to those of interests, although the evidence is not so complete as the evidence about interests. Need, which perhaps reflects a more basic aspect of personality, has been related to explanations of vocational behavior primarily in theories of vocational development, but the empirical evidence is not yet impressive.

Trait, a term that refers to a consistency in behavior, is a general construct of which the variables of interest, value, and need might be considered some of the specific components. Emphasizing aptitudes, interests, and other such variables, the trait-and-factor approach has provided much of the basic data in occupational psychology. As advances in theory are made, more comprehensive explanations of the role of traits in occupations are being developed. In addition, the trait-and-factor approach may be helpful in the understanding of factors that cut across occupations, such as *style*, which focuses on the mode, rather than the content, of behavior.

Self-concept is a summary personality description that explicitly takes into account the person's picture of himself. Self-concept theory and methodology have been extensively used in current theories of vocational development and have been particularly useful in relating personality to occupations: people tend to choose occupations that they construe as representing the characteristics they see in themselves.

part three

Career Development

It is easy to fall into the error of thinking that occupational psychology is simply a matter of individual differences, of tests, and of the application of these differences and these tests to occupational choice and selection. This type of thinking exists largely because, by accident, the objective study of individual differences developed early, and the methods of studying the sequence of positions occupied by a given person during the course of his working life developed late.

Narrowly defined, occupational psychology is, indeed, largely a matter of individual differences. But broadly defined, if the term *occupational* is treated as synonymous with *vocational,* occupational psychology is more than just applied individual differences. An occupation is what a person does, a vocation is what he feels called upon to do, and a career is the sequence of things he does to earn a living.

We are concerned here with a broad definition, because we are concerned with the application of psychology to the individual's choice of work, success in work, and satisfaction in work. Part Three, therefore, examines in some detail, in its first chapter, the concepts of occupations and careers, defining them from psychological and sociological perspectives. It points out the *developmental* nature of a psychology of careers, as contrasted with the *differential* emphasis of occupational psychology. Occupational and career models are described, and three studies of career development are discussed in some detail.

In the second chapter of Part Three, the concept of life stages is developed, the distinctive characteristics of each stage are noted, and various kinds of career patterns are described. Occupational choice is described as a process of self-actualization engaged in by a choosing person, and studies of this process are reviewed.

chapter six

Occupations
versus
Careers

The terms "occupation" and "career" are often used as though they were synonyms, but they actually have rather different meanings, which have become confused in everyday usage. The reasons for the confusion are understandable, but it is important to avoid the confusion.

An occupation is a type of work activity in which people engage, a group of similar tasks organized in similar ways in various establishments, an activity that has a market value and in which people are, therefore, paid to engage. Viewed *economically*, an occupation is a means of assuring the performance of necessary work and thus also of securing a steady flow of income to individuals. Viewed *sociologically*, an occupation is a role with certain socially defined expectations, played in a network of related roles that constitute the systems of production, distribution, and service, for certain generally expected material and psychic rewards. Viewed *psychologically*, an occupation is a set of tasks and role expectations, the performance or meeting of which requires certain skills, knowledges, aptitudes, and interests and brings certain rewards.

A career, by contrast, is the sequence of occupations, jobs, and positions engaged in or occupied throughout the lifetime of a person. Viewed *economically*, a career is a series of positions occupied by a person as a means of preparing to earn, earning, or withdrawing from the earning of a livelihood. Viewed *sociologically*, it is a series of roles played by a person, in which the nature of each role played, the way in which it is played, and the situation in which it is played have some bearing on the nature of the next role in the series. Viewed *psychologically*, a career is also a series of roles played by a person, the choice of and success in which are determined in part by the aptitudes, interests, values, needs, prior experiences, and expectations of the person in question. A person may change occupations more than once during his working life: Winston Churchill, for example, was a newspaper reporter before becoming a politician and a cabinet minister; William James was successively a physician, philosopher, and psychologist; and Herbert Hoover was an engineer, a public administrator, and a statesman. Even in pursuing the same occupation for some time, as many people do, there are usually several changes of jobs or positions as people are promoted, transferred, discharged, or attracted by better opportunities in other departments, in other companies, or in other localities.

The two terms, occupation and career, are often confused because people have a tendency, in certain well-known occupations, to achieve a substantial degree of stability over time. Physicians usually choose their profession in their late teens, prepare for it in their early twenties, become established in it not long before they are thirty, and pursue it for the rest of their working lives, even though many cease to *practice* medicine in the usual sense of the word and instead become medical administrators, researchers, manufacturers, or publicists. Such stability is also characteristic, although to a lesser extent, of lawyers, engineers, teachers, and members of other professions, preparation for which involves a substantial investment of time and money: the greater the investment, the greater the stability in the occupation. The relationship between length and expense of preparation and occupational stability is shown in the tendency of the professions that require the shortest periods of training, demand the least specialization, and offer the least inducement to continue in the profession to lose large proportions of their graduates to other occupations: teaching is the prime example. The career of many women employed in the *occupation* of teacher is actually best embodied in the *vocation* of housewife!

It is not just in the professions that occupation and career are often truly synonymous. In the skilled trades, continuity of people in one occupation throughout most of their working careers is also common. Here too the investment of time and money in preparation for the occupation and the financial and social rewards for remaining in it are great enough to assure the stability of many who complete training.

But in many other occupations, the period of preparation is not long enough, the field in which the skills and knowledge are acquired is not specific enough, or the rewards for remaining in the occupation are not great enough to assure the continuity of those trained for the occupation in that field of work. For many executives and for many managerial, clerical, sales, semiskilled, and unskilled workers, a career involves a series of moves from one occupation to another. For some, there is continuity in the industry in which work is found. For example, a man in the furniture industry may work his way from an entry job requiring only a few hours of orientation through a series of other jobs in the industry, and in due course he may be an expert on the production of wooden or "case" goods, of upholstered furniture, or both. For others, the only continuity is that of the life of the worker, as he changes from deck hand on an ore boat in the summer to operative in a tire factory during the winter, moves on in search of better wages in an automobile factory, and then seeks freedom from the assembly line as a gas-station attendant. Such varied employment is found not only at the semiskilled level, but, as noted above, at the clerical, sales, executive, and even occasionally the professional levels. It is well, then, to keep clear the distinction between *occupation* (what one does) and *career* (the course pursued over a period of time).

Differential versus Developmental Psychology

A DIFFERENTIAL PSYCHOLOGY OF VOCATIONS

Occupational psychology was, from its beginnings early in this century until quite recently, essentially a psychology of occupations rather than of careers. Although often called vocational psychology, it dealt with vocation as a synonym for occupation, for a type of work done by a person. It focused on the occupation. Insofar as the people who engaged in the occupation were considered, it was as the possessors of aptitudes, interests, and personality traits that contributed to success or satisfaction in the work. Occupational psychology was the differential psychology of occupations.

Differential occupational psychology began, we have seen, with the study of the intelligence of soldiers coming from various civilian occupations. This work led to the study of special aptitudes such as manual dexterity, spatial visualization, and perceptual speed and accuracy in relation to mechanical and clerical occupations. One project began as a study of the human resources brought in by immigration from Europe (72). It paved the way for a landmark study of abilities, unemployment, and reemployment (73). This study in turn led to the development of the *General Aptitude Test Battery* of the United States Employment Service (83) and with it the means of assessing the aptitudes of new workers against the standards of a great variety of entry jobs. As occupational ability patterns were being studied, another trend, first under the leadership of one man (88) and eventually with the work of many others, led to the development of interest inventories, which established the existence of and made possible the measurement of occupational interest patterns.

These developments and other more recent examples such as the Thorndike and Hagen study (101), *Project Talent* (34), and the Minnesota work on vocational interests (21, 18) were discussed in Chapters 4 and 5. Occupational ability and interest profiles and the instruments for measuring them have made possible the matching of men and jobs in vocational counseling and in personnel selection; such matching is discussed in more detail in Chapters 8 and 9, but a brief explanation of the method and its use will be helpful here.

THE OCCUPATIONAL MODEL

The matching of men and jobs was a much more popular concept in 1940 (7), when the possibilities of vocational testing first became a reality, than it is now, when the complexities of men and of work are clearer. The problem of vocational guidance and personnel selection had been formulated as one of predicting occupational success. The method that had emerged was that of relating pre-employment test scores to later success. In such a formulation, the researcher and the practitioner deal with status at two points in time, implying that these are the only times of interest and importance. In matching men and jobs, the assumption is that, once the match is well made, happiness ever after will be the result. Problems of training and of job-getting, of human malleability and mobility, and of industrial change are disregarded. That training is often required, that jobs may be plentiful or scarce, that people change with time, and that work changes too were of course generally recognized but were not taken into account by the occupational model.

Despite its shortcomings, the occupational model is useful. People do differ in ways that can be measured, and these differences are important in occupational choice, success, and satisfaction. Tests of known occupational validity, used by a well-trained counselor, promote better vocational counseling, as shown by various measures of the outcomes of counseling (73, 27, 17).

For example, by examining the aptitude and interest profile of a young man or woman wondering for which of several occupations to prepare or which of several jobs to take, a counselor can help his client to see how well equipped he is to compete with those whom he will encounter in his training or in his work, how much he has in common with those with whom he will be associated, and how congenial he will find the activities in which he would engage. Other factors need to be considered also, including resources available for training, family support for a given choice, and employment opportunities. Tests and inventories throw light on the psychological goodness of fit of occupational choices, a consideration that is important, though not sufficient to determine by itself a person's occupational choice.

It is not surprising, then, that differential psychology became the foundation of occupational psychology, that vocational psychology adopted an occupational model, and that the counseling services of many schools, colleges, and community agencies put heavy emphasis on the use of the readily usable psychometric tools.

A Developmental Psychology of Vocations

A career is a sequence of positions, "a course of continued progress in the life of a person," as Webster defines it. It clearly involves the concept of development. One position leads vertically or laterally, directly or indirectly, systematically or haphazardly, to another position. The progress may not be up a career ladder on which people climb from one rung to the next in "a course of progressive achievement," as Webster clarifies another nuance, but whatever move is made at one point in a career is to some degree an outcome of positions occupied earlier in the career. Occupying the position of student in an engineering school may lead to working as a production engineer some years later, but the position of elevator operator in a department store is not likely to lead to an engineering position.

Careers begin before employment, and they are shaped by parental background through its determination of exposure to occupations and educational opportunities, by aptitudes and interests, and by educational attainments. Careers extend into retirement, as the man on a pension seeks and finds things to do: the things he does are occupations in the sense of organized tasks that structure life and give it meaning. Careers might be described as consisting of *preparing* for roles, *playing* roles, and *relinquishing* roles, with work roles in the center of the adult stage in modern industrialized economies, particularly for men. In the study and in the guidance of careers, the emphasis is on the continuities and discontinuities in life (91, 103, 60). The objectives of study and guidance are to help increase the continuity of development along sound lines and to minimize the likelihood and the negative effects of discontinuity resulting from injury, economic loss, and obsolescence.

THE CAREER MODEL

The career model in developmental vocational psychology is a descriptive model. In it, the individual is viewed as moving along one of a number of possible pathways from his family position in the socioeconomic system, through the grades of the educational system, and into and through the jobs of the work system. The model provides norms of typical behavior and of its determinants. The starting point is the father's socioeconomic status. From there, the individual climbs a certain distance up the educational ladder at a speed determined partly by personal (psychological and social) characteristics, partly by environmental (economic, political, and social) characteristics, and partly by the active interventions of teachers, counselors, and employers. He enters the world of work at a point that is fixed in part by the rung on the educational ladder he has reached at the time of leaving school for work. He progresses through an entry job into one or more other jobs, which may or may not be related to each other as the rungs on a ladder. Career prediction, understanding where and how a person is likely to move from the position he now occupies, is what many vocational counselors attempt in practice despite the lack of scientific tools. It is the essence of vocational counseling when more is involved than a decision about a specific job. But counselors have so far had little in the way of theory, data, and tools to help understand the direction and probability of movement. Those data and tools that are available fit the occupational, not the career, model.

The career model takes into account the sequence of occupations, jobs, and positions that a given person is *likely* to occupy. It is not necessary to attempt to predict the whole sequence of positions from the cradle to the grave, or even from high school to retirement. Neither is the *likely* to be accepted as the *necessary*: counselors are, *de jure* if not always *de facto*, interventionists. But it will be of great practical value to have a better understanding of the nature and determinants of sequences, together with a systematic organization of these data, to facilitate the prediction of the academic positions and the early occupational positions of a career and to highlight needed intervention.

The occupational model takes predictor data at an early stage of the career and uses statistical methods to predict later success in one occupation, or uses other methods of analysis as a means of assessing the goodness of fit in each of several possible occupations. That the subject may hold several different positions at successive ages is disregarded. The prediction of success in engineering, accounting, or sales at some time in adulthood is treated as though a position in one of these fields, at one particular moment in time, were the equivalent of a career, of an adult lifetime.

The occupational-prediction model uses statistical methods that are quite appropriate for prediction from one point to one other point in time. But such methods are only now being adapted to prediction from one point to a whole series of later points in time.

The prediction method that appears to be most promising is that of *Markov chains* (61, 43), which had previously been used in studying games and policy-making behavior. This model makes it possible to estimate the probability that a young man or woman who occupies a given position or who engages in a given kind of vocational behavior at one point will manifest a given kind of behavior at a later point and that this later behavior is similarly linked to behavior at one or more still later stages. These links constitute a chain showing the relationships of status and position over time. Gribbons and Lohnes found that the probability that a boy or girl who is floundering vocationally—that is, unaware of and uninformed about careers—in the eighth grade will continue that way in the tenth grade is about two to one, from tenth grade to twelfth grade it is about the same, from twelfth grade to two years after graduation it is three to one, and for the whole period from eighth grade until two years after high school it is not quite two to one. This suggests that, during the teens, those who have clear-cut goals at one time tend to have them at other times, and that those who are unsure of their objectives at one time are likely to be unsure at others. The greatest apparent degree of consistency in this type of vocational behavior is found from twelfth grade to two years later, the flounderers at the earlier time being most likely to keep on floundering, and those who had clear-cut goals at the earlier date being most likely still to have them two years later. This continuity, this linkage of vocational coping behavior, may continue beyond that point, or major discontinuities may appear as many college students find that their preliminary choice of major was not appropriate: the stability of those who appeared not to be floundering may prove to have been a false stability.

Three Vocational Development Studies

Three ongoing longitudinal studies of career development well illustrate the current theories and methods. They are described below as studies, as prime examples of how psychological research is conducted and of an important new trend in occupational psychology. Other important work not discussed here is described in Borow (15).

The Career Pattern Study

The Career Pattern Study (96) was begun in 1951 in an attempt to forge a developmental theory of vocational choice and success while collecting and analyzing data that would make possible empirically based descriptions of the choice and adjustment process. Some 200 boys in ninth grade in 1951 and 1952 were interviewed and tested several times—at the beginning of the Career Pattern Study (CPS), as they finished high school, and again when they were about 25 years old—in an intensive study of their characteristics and experiences. Their parents were also interviewed, and an analysis was made of employment and of occupational opportunities in the area.

The goal of the study was to describe the development of careers. More specifically, there were two objectives: the definition and measurement of vocational maturity from early adolescence until adulthood and the development of criteria of vocational success that are appropriate to young men approaching adulthood and involved in the process of getting established in adult occupations.

VOCATIONAL MATURITY

Vocational maturity is shown by behavior in coping with the tasks of vocational development that is mature compared with that of others dealing with the same tasks. Boys and girls of a given age face similar demands from the organization of schools and their curricula: the ninth grade is a point of choice, at which certain decisions have to be made if the pupil is to stay in the system.

In the Career Pattern Study, findings about ninth-grade boys that are particularly significant have to do with the nature, degree, and causes or concomitants of vocational maturity. First, indices of vocational maturity widely used in counseling, such as consistency and realism of preferences, do not show the relationships that could be expected among measures of the same basic variable, whereas novel indices assessing the ability to plan and the time perspective of the ninth-grade boys *are* intercorrelated. Second, the level of vocational development attained in ninth grade is not sufficiently high to make sound vocational decisions possible. That is, the understanding of the self, of education, or of the world of work that a person has reached by ninth grade does not justify his deciding on courses leading toward one occupational field rather than toward others. Third, vocational maturity is related to ability, to having had opportunities to develop interests and to use abilities, and to the habit of taking advantage of these opportunities.

Vocational maturity in the twelfth grade has also been studied as a trait and as a predictor of success and satisfaction in young adulthood. Factor analysis shows that the structure of vocational maturity in the twelfth grade is very similar to that in ninth grade.

The stability of vocational maturity as a trait is considerably lower than that of aptitudes such as intelligence and spatial visualization. Maturing vocationally appears to be an uneven and irregular process, the status of individuals in a group varying on such traits as tendency to plan ahead, acceptance of responsibility, and awareness of contingencies as it varies on other personality traits in adolescence.

As they get older, boys learn more about the occupations in which they are interested. They get jobs in which they are more independent than they were when they were younger, they have clearer and more definite ideas of what they want to do as adults, and they are more aware of alternative vocational plans. Only one-sixth of the CPS twelfth-graders had the same occupational preference they had in ninth grade, one-twentieth aspired to a different occupation in the same field but at a different level, and more than one-half were interested in occupations in quite different fields. More than two-thirds of the CPS twelfth-grade boys did not feel at all committed to the occupations in which they said they were most interested.

These findings, in both ninth and twelfth grade, show that the high school years are essentially years of vocational exploration rather than of preparation for an occupation. They are years in which young people learn much about the world of work and about fitting into it, but in which most youth do not, in fact, choose a life work. They do well if they succeed in laying the foundations for a sound choice by learning about occupations and about the implications of their own abilities and interests for the series of choices with which they are confronted as they go through school and enter the labor force.

SUCCESS IN THE TWENTIES

Success has a traditional meaning. When *occupational* prediction is attempted, the criterion of success is naturally one of success in the occupation entered. The measure of success may therefore be a rating by a supervisor or a record of the output or earnings of the worker: thus, to obtain a measure of success, Strong (88) found out how much insurance was later sold by the men who had taken his interest inventory when applying for insurance sales jobs. From a broader perspective, success may be defined as stability in the occupation or ratings by others in the profession who know the work of the person being rated: thus one study asked judges to rate the success of lawyers practicing in their courts.

But in the study of *career* success, especially in young people, occupational criteria may not be appropriate. Instead of using a measure of success in whatever occupation a person happens to be engaged in at the time, it may be better to use measures of success that reflect how well he is handling the task of finding and getting established in an appropriate occupation.

An attempt to strike a balance led the people involved in the Career Pattern Study to develop and use both occupational and career success measures (97). Several measures of career success and satisfaction can serve to illustrate those that were tried.

Career moves, a person's changes of position as student or as worker after leaving high school, can be conceived of as involving either *floundering* or *stabilizing*. Floundering is haphazard movement, while stabilizing is trying out something that appears appropriate, doing something that will make possible the attainment of a goal, or getting established in an appropriate field of work. In the CPS, each move was judged by trained psychologists who studied data from the subjects' educational and work histories. The measures showed whether each move, the typical move, and the latest move in a person's history involved floundering or stabilizing.

Career moves can also be studied by means of ratings of the *realism of reasons* for changing positions. In the CPS, one score thus obtained was an average for all of the moves in a person's post–high school history.

Another criterion measure, *occupational success*, can be rated by the individual himself. In the CPS, such ratings were found, despite the inherent defects of self-rating, to be reasonably valid.

Finally, a measure of the *number of moves* or position changes can be constructed by simply counting changes, and the *occupational level* of the most recent job can be rated. Table 6–1 shows the intercorrelations of these success criteria in the Career Pattern Study.

TABLE 6–1. *Intercorrelations of career and occupational criteria.**†

	Stabilizing	Realism	Success	Level	Moves
Stabilizing vs. Floundering	—	.30	.27	.46	−.12
Realism of Reasons	—	—	.27	.36	−.35
Occupational Success	—		—	.26	−.18
Occupational Level	-			—	−.01

* Numbers vary from 88 to 116; underlined correlations are significant at the .01 level of probability; none were significant at only the .05 level.
† Super, D. E., Kowalski, R. S., and Gotkin, E. H. Floundering and trial after high school. Cooperative Research Project No. 1393. New York: Teachers College, Columbia University, 1967.

The CPS measures of stabilizing, realism of reasons for changing positions, self-estimated occupational success, and occupational level attained by age 25 are all positively interrelated. It is not unexpected that those who work at the higher occupational levels are more stable, for these are the occupations that tend to be entered after appropriate college or university preparation and that offer the greatest job and financial security. That realism of reasons for changing is substantially correlated with level may also be a function of the type of job, rather than of the kind of person holding it. It is noteworthy that while both of the career criteria (stabilizing and realism) are positively related to the occupational criteria (occupational success and level), only one of these is related to number of moves or position changes: those who move most tend to have the least realistic reasons for moving ($r = -.35$).

THE ANTECEDENTS OF SUCCESS

Another task of the Career Pattern Study has been to examine the relationships between antecedent and criterion variables—that is, between characteristics of boys in junior and senior high school and their success in their middle twenties. Table 6–2 reports some of the findings.

TABLE 6–2. *Correlations between 12th grade characteristics and young adult success.**†

	Vocational Maturity	Stabilizing at Age 25	Realism of Reasons for Changing	Occ'l Success	Occ'l Level	Number of Moves
Information: Education for Preferred Occupation	.33	.32	—.05	.40	—.14
Agreement: Abilities Possessed and Required	.19	.14	.19	.07	.01
Standard Measures: Intelligence	.28	.29	.22	.41	—.05
High School Grades	.28	.53	.24	.44	—.21
School Activities	.25	.28	.21	.44	—.07

* Correlations underlined once are significant at the .05 level of probability; twice, at the .01 level.

† Super, D. E., Kowalski, R. S., and Gotkin, E. H. Floundering and trial after high school. Cooperative Research Project No. 1393. New York: Teachers College, Columbia University, 1967.

A number of possible measures of vocational maturity were tried out. Of these, the measure of *information concerning education and training needed* for the occupation in which one was then most interested appeared to be one of the best empirical measures in both ninth and twelfth grades. As Table 6–2 shows, it proved also to be one of the best predictors of success in young adulthood: knowing something in twelfth grade about how to prepare for the preferred occupation is related to stabilizing rather than floundering at age 25, to realism of reasons for changing positions during the years after leaving high school, and to the level attained on the occupational ladder. Although not shown in this table, the ninth grade scores tended to predict as did the twelfth, but with the less substantial and less frequent validities that would be expected at an earlier age.

The degree of *agreement between the abilities possessed and those required* by the preferred occupation did not, in ninth grade, appear to be a sound measure of vocational maturity, for it was not related to other measures in the anticipated ways. However, in twelfth grade it appeared to be a more meaningful measure, as confirmed by its tendency to have low but positive relationships to the success criteria of stabilizing and occupational success. That the correlations are as low as .19 and barely significant statistically suggests that this kind of realism is still not a practically useful measure, even in twelfth graders.

Of the several standard measures frequently used in schools, only three will be discussed here. *Intelligence* and *grade-point average*, themselves positively intercorrelated, both correlate with stabilizing, realism of reasons for changing positions, occupational success, and occupational level. Grades, however, correlate negatively with the number of moves made after leaving high school. The number of position changes did not prove to be a generally predictable criterion of success, and it is therefore perhaps not meaningful. Nonetheless, it does seem that students who get better grades tend to make fewer position changes than those who get poorer grades. This could be because good students go to college, do well there, and therefore make few changes of position. Poorer students, on the other hand, either get jobs that are necessarily marginal because of their age and education on leaving high school or go to college and do poorly there. In either case, they change positions (jobs or majors) more often. The amount and the quality of participation in *school activities* tend to have the same kind of predictive validity as grades do.

FLOUNDERING AND STABILIZING

The concepts of floundering and stabilizing can be broken down into more specific types of behavior. Changes of educational or vocational positions can be classified according to the quality of the coping behavior. CPS categories are floundering (chance), trial (systematic), instrumental (means to an end), establishing (starting in an appropriate position), or stagnating (staying in an inappropriate position).

More than half of the position changes between leaving school and age 25 are of the floundering or aimless variety; about one-third are considered trial in that they are clearly purposive. Much smaller numbers of moves involve getting established in an appropriate occupation or are instrumental in that they lead to another, appropriate goal. When the most recent job changes made during the years after high school and before age 25 are classified as involving stabilizing (trial, instrumental, or establishing) or floundering behavior, about 80 percent of the subjects are found to be engaging in stabilizing—that is, in positive coping behaviors—at age 25. About half of these had stabilized without much earlier floundering. It is noteworthy that many of the other half, those whose early vocational coping behavior involved floundering, are nevertheless stabilizing at age 25. One-fifth of them, however, are still making haphazard moves. The average number of position changes during the seven years after leaving high school, including student and work positions, is six, nearly one change per year.

The Career Development Study

A longitudinal study of 111 eighth-grade boys and girls, using modifications of some of the procedures of the Career Pattern Study, was begun by Gribbons and Lohnes in 1958. They used an interview schedule or questionnaire in the eighth, tenth, and twelfth grades and again in a follow-up two years after high school. All of the subjects were reached at all stages, largely in interviews, but the questionnaire was administered by mail in a few cases. The subjects were a selected sample of 57 boys and 54 girls in small cities near Boston.

VOCATIONAL MATURITY

Readiness for Vocational Planning (RVP) scales were constructed from the scoring of the interview material. The first two scales, factors in curriculum choice and factors in occupational choice, include material covered in the Career Pattern Study (CPS) information and planning indices, but add consideration of the accuracy of the information. A scale measuring awareness of the relevance of interests and values and another assessing independence of choice also resemble CPS indices of wisdom of preferences and indices of acceptance of responsibility for choice and planning. The other scales measure verbalized strengths and weaknesses, accuracy of self-appraisal, and amount of evidence for self-rating. Although the scales are relatively independent or only moderately intercorrelated, they have one general underlying factor (supporting the hypothesized underlying construct of vocational maturity) and reflect at least three other less important factors.

RVP scores increased from eighth to tenth grade, suggesting that the scales do indeed measure vocational maturity. There was considerable overlapping of eighth- and tenth-grade scores. Some stability in RVP profiles was shown by moderate correlations between eighth and tenth grade scores, suggesting that vocational development is not an altogether uneven process in the early teens. The scale of factors in occupational choice was the one variable that did not show such stability; that is, it was the educational and psychological variables, rather than the vocational, that proved stable. The CDS results are thus more similar to the CPS findings than they appear to be at first inspection.

The CDS findings, however, differ in some important respects from those of the CPS. Readiness for vocational planning in the eighth grade has as much predictive validity for curriculum choice and level of occupational preference as it does when assessed two and one-half years later. RVP in eighth grade is a better predictor of twelfth-grade educational and occupational planning than is RVP in tenth grade. Readiness in eighth grade also gives better predictions of educational and occupational levels, field and level of actual occupation two years after high school, and post–high school career adjustment. That tenth-grade RVP is less dependent on verbal ability and less homogeneous, and therefore appears more discriminating, makes its lower predictive validity surprising. Unlike the CPS indices, RVP scores showed no appreciable relationship to socioeconomic status.

As a measure of vocational maturity (increasing with age, becoming less dependent on verbal ability, and differentiating increasingly well with increasing age), tenth-grade Readiness for Vocational Planning should be a better predictor than eighth-grade RVP of twelfth-grade and post–high school characteristics. Maturing traits generally yield better predictions after they have increased with maturity. When there are differences in predictive value, the measures taken closer to the criterion date tend to be the better. As RVP Scales do not conform to this rule, they clearly need further study and may be inadequate scales.

Differential career processes were also studied by Gribbons and Lohnes. They identified as *emerging maturity* the process involved in sequentially manifesting the types of coping behavior identified by Super and associates (floundering, trial, stagnating, instrumental, and establishing). Additional career processes include *constant maturity,* the consistent and persistent pursuit of the goal first stated; *degeneration,* the progressive deterioration of aspirations and achievement; and *constant immaturity,* fixation on unrealistic goals without advance in level of achievement. Nearly half of the students of each sex had secondary school careers that fell into the *emerging maturity* category, less than a third of each sex were found to show *degeneration,* more than one-tenth of the boys and one-fifth of the girls showed *constant maturity,* and one-fifth of the boys and one-tenth of the girls showed *constant immaturity.*

Success ratings, made two years after high school graduation on the basis of a comparison between high school aspirations and actual employment, showed that less than half of the boys were successful in achieving high school goals, a slightly larger number unsuccessful, and about one-sixth occupationally neutral (in military service). Girls were more frequently unsuccessful in attaining high school goals: more than one-third were successful in maintaining desired careers, more than one-half were not maintaining careers desired in high school, and one-tenth were neutral (not in civilian gainful employment, largely housewives). Success was found to be related to differential career processes such as emerging maturity and constant immaturity while in high school.

Readiness for vocational planning (vocational maturity) in junior and senior high school, as assessed by Gribbons and Lohnes, had no relationship to concurrent differential career processes or behaviors. The results of their assessment were so at odds with theory and with other evidence that Gribbons and Lohnes reject them, expecting positive results in future studies. Caution does seem warranted in evaluating pioneer studies such as these.

The Markov chain model was applied by Gribbons and Lohnes to some of their longitudinal data. They related coping behavior at one point in time to that at the next point in time in a series of links and summarized these links in a chain covering the whole of adolescence. The career-development process is clearly not random or haphazard.

Project Talent

In 1960, a comprehensive battery of aptitude and achievement tests, interest and personality inventories, and biographical questionnaires was administered at several grade levels in a longitudinal study of 440,000 boys and girls who constitute a representative sample of 5 percent of American high school students. John Flanagan and associates (32) at the American Institute for Research collected data from the schools on their guidance programs, curricula, and staff. Follow-up has been done periodically since then to keep the educational and vocational histories of the subjects up to date. Major objectives of the project include analyses of the determinants of vocational plans and choices and of the distribution and use of talents. Trait-and-factor data are used in studying career development, which so far involves plans or preferences rather than fully implemented choices (33).

THE DETERMINANTS OF CAREERS

The High School Student (33) reports a vast amount of data from the basic Project Talent study and the one-year follow-up of twelfth graders. Career plans are developed in various ways. Sixteen percent of the twelfth-grade boys planned to become engineers, and 12.5 percent of the same boys followed up one year later still planned to become engineers and were enrolled in first-year engineering courses. By contrast, only 7 percent of the twelfth-grade boys planned to enter the field of education, but 12 percent of the same group were preparing for it a year later. About 42 percent of the high school graduates went on to college, 22 percent of the college students dropping out during the first year. Business and commercial majors were most popular, but engineering ranked second for boys, and education highest for girls. Among students going directly to work after high school, most jobs were semiskilled, low-level service, factory, and clerical jobs viewed as temporary.

Some of the expected occupational aptitude patterns were found: higher *technical* than *academic* aptitude test scores were made by electricians, mechanics, and gas-station attendants. However, in some cases a pattern was lacking: girl office workers differed little in aptitude patterns from girls in general.

Ability and *family socioeconomic level* were found, in a later report of the *One Year Follow-Up Studies* of all 440,000 boys and girls (34), to be major determinants of post–high school education. Junior college students tended to be more like non-college students than like four-year college students in ability, but more like the college-going group in family socioeconomic level.

Of the pupils first studied in ninth grade, 68 percent continued their education after high school: 49 percent went on to college, 38 percent to four-year and 11 percent to junior colleges. The college dropout rate was 19 percent. One year after leaving high school, 63 percent of the non-college boys in the 1960 class, 74 percent of the non-college boys graduating in 1961, and 83 percent of the non-college boys graduating in 1962 were employed full-time. The largest occupational groups, employing from about 10 percent to about 25 percent of the boys, were the clerical and semiskilled. The clerical and sales field accounted for 75 percent of the girls, followed by the service field with 10 percent to 15 percent. Dropouts were typically less well placed than graduates.

The stability of career plans during the high school years and one year after was low: only 17 percent of the ninth-grade boys had the same occupational goal one year after high school. This percentage rose to 19 percent, 25 percent, and 31 percent for preferences expressed in the succeeding grades. The percentages for girls were only a little higher. From the poor predictions of later preferences from earlier occupational preferences, Flanagan concluded that other more stable data, such as those provided by tests, must be relied upon more heavily in counseling.

ABILITY AND MOTIVATION

Using a six-category occupational classification, Cooley showed that grouped occupational preferences are much more stable than specific occupational preferences. Thus, when grouped preferences were used, plans one year after high school were predicted as well by ninth-grade preferences as by ability and motivation measures. Motivation measures were better predictors than ability measures, but the ability measures increased in predictive validity while the motivation measures decreased during the high school years. The ability and interest scores of those boys who changed plans from ninth grade to one year after high school were compared with those of boys who did not change. Figure 6–1 graphically and dramatically reveals the results.

Students who changed plans from physical science to technical occupations (coded as 5. PS-TE in Figure 6–1) made much lower scores on scholastic aptitude tests (the horizontal axis in Figure 6–1) than did those retaining such aspirations in the first year after high school (coded as 1. Physical Science), but were no lower on the mathematical-mechanical tests (the vertical axis). Students who shifted from the physical science to the business (non-college) field (coded 6. PS-BNC) were lower on both types of aptitude. Similar trends existed for interests, which were similarly analyzed, but to a lesser degree. For example, students who first planned to enter the humanities, but shifted to business administration, scored a little higher on physical science and

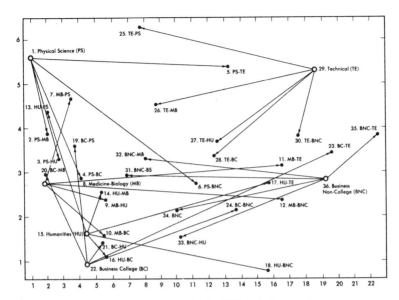

FIGURE 6–1. *Project TALENT ability and interest scores of boys in grade 9 and one year after high school: The 36 centroids in the ability space.* John C. Flanagan and William W. Cooley, Project TALENT: One Year Follow-up Studies. Pittsburgh: University of Pittsburgh Press, 1966. Reprinted by permission.

technical interests and a little lower on scholastic interests than those who continued to plan on careers in the humanities.

The response rate has been a problem in Project Talent, for the methods used in getting 90 percent to 100 percent returns in intensive studies of small samples, such as the Career Pattern and Career Development Studies, are not practical in massive projects such as this. The returns for the first-year post–high school follow-up in Project Talent range from 37 percent for the original ninth graders to 69 percent for the original twelfth graders, using systematic waves of questionnaires and cards. If adequate returns are obtained—and whether they will be is a major question—information on sequences of full-time occupations (that is, careers) will provide more meaningful criteria than the vocational plans and training criteria necessarily used so far in Project Talent.

Summary

The basic difference between an occupation and a career is the longitudinal, sequential character of the latter as opposed to the static nature of the former. An occupation is what one does to earn a living at some one point in time, whereas a career is the sequence of positions occupied over a period of time.

Occupational psychology has traditionally focused on occupations, drawing on differential psychology to throw light on the characteristics of people in various occupations and on the determinants of success in these occupations. The occupational model of choice was one of matching individual traits with those of people engaged in the occupation. The introduction of a developmental approach to occupational choice led to the concept of career or vocational development. It also led to the use of a career model in which the focus is on the characteristics of persons pursuing differing sequences of educational and occupational positions and on the nature of those sequences.

Three studies of career development were discussed in some detail. These were the Career Pattern Study of a typical group of some 200 boys from junior high school into the Establishment Stage, the Career Development Study of about 100 boys and girls from junior high school into young adulthood, both of which deal with vocational maturity and career processes, and the large-scale Project Talent study of the determinants of plans and of their attainment. The Career Pattern Study's measures of vocational maturity, as evidenced by information about the occupation preferred while in school and by achievement in school tasks as shown by grades and by school activities, were seen to have some relationship to success in young adulthood when success is judged by the realism of reasons for changing positions, self-estimated occupational success, the number of changes of positions, and global ratings of floundering or stabilizing career behavior.

The Career Development Study used some measures of vocational maturity that resembled those of the older Career Pattern Study, but it also developed some that were novel. Its readiness-for-vocational-planning scales showed some predictive validity from eighth to tenth grade, but did not predict the differential handling of career processes such as floundering, although floundering in school did predict success as measured by the later attainment of high school goals.

Project Talent has made an important contribution in reporting on the relationships between aptitudes and interests tested in high school and later occupation as shown by professional study and by early employment history. Aptitudes appear as more important determinants than interests in this analysis, but, as usual, socioeconomic status plays a major role in career development. In developing a Career Tree as a graphic portrayal of career development, and in supplementing this portrayal with data on the traits of those who enter and leave each pre-vocational and vocational group, Flanagan and Cooley have made a major contribution to modern occupational psychology.

The next chapter completes the discussion of career development with consideration of life stages and career patterns.

chapter seven

How Careers
Unfold

Careers are rarely chosen by a person who, in high school or college, surveys the future and plots his course ahead through the years. Some students do approximate this procedure, as when a high school senior decides to prepare to be a physician and to enter practice with his father, or when a young man enters the family-owned manufacturing business with the expectation of eventually managing the factory. For most people, however, the steps they will go through in their careers are somewhat unclear; they move by successive approximations toward a place in the world of work. It is the objective of this chapter to clarify these steps, drawing on theory and research on life stages, on career patterns, on developmental tasks, and on the role of self-concepts in vocational development.

Life Stages and Careers

The Human Life Span

Poets, dramatists, biographers, economists, philosophers, sociologists, and psychologists have long made use of the concept of life stages. The problems of rearing children, getting started in an occupation, and aging have made the man in the street conscious of the varying stages through which people go as they progress through childhood, into adolescence and adulthood, and on into old age. When Shakespeare wrote of the seven ages of man, he wrote of experiences familiar to all of his readers. When behavioral scientists began to study the human life span and to analyze its components and determinants, they chose a topic full of meaning to most of the persons participating in their studies. In studying life in general, the behavioral scientists encountered many activities that are occupational or occupationally determined. In vocational psychology, the typical procedure has been to develop a record of the work histories of a sample of the people whose careers are to be studied. This record may list all of the positions occupied, including those of child in a certain kind of home, pupil in various types of schools, head of a household of changing size and ages, worker in a series of different occupations, and pensioner retired from work and from community activity. On the other hand, the record may be limited to part of the life-span and to certain kinds of positions. In either case, it may go beyond mere analysis of the sequence and duration of positions to analyses of the types of problems faced at the various life stages and of the factors influencing their handling. Five life stages tend to stand out in this type of analysis (92, 96): childhood, adolescence, young adulthood, maturity, and old age. Table 7-1 describes them.

CHILDHOOD

The first stage, childhood, is one of physical, psychological, and social *growth*. The child grows not only in stature and in strength, but in cognitive capacity, in emotional stability and maturity, and in social skills and adjustment. Once he enters school, he adds rapidly to his ability to work and play with a variety of people, and he masters the skills of communication and of calculation. He develops ideas about what he *can* do, what he *likes* to do, and what others *expect* him to do: his self-concept begins to take form. Vocationally, he acquires concepts of a number of occupations, including those engaged in by his parents, his neighbors, and the people about whom he hears or reads in books, in television programs, and in class. The child relates concepts of self as boy or girl to concepts of occupations, some of which he sees as appropriate for men, others for women, and others for both sexes.

Much of a child's thinking about himself in vocational terms is based on immature needs: the need for affection and the desire to be strong and powerful tend to make small boys identify with and seek to emulate their fathers. As they grow older and learn more about other men and their work, they shift their *identification* accordingly. They find other heroes who are admired by their friends. The little girl sees homemaking as woman's major role. The child imagines

TABLE 7–1. *Vocational life stages.**

---

1. *Growth Stage* (Birth–14)

Self-concept develops through identification with key figures in family and in school; needs and fantasy are dominant early in this stage; interest and capacity become more important in this stage with increasing social participation and reality-testing. Substages of the growth stage are:

FANTASY (4–10). Needs are dominant; role-playing in fantasy is important.

INTERESTS (11–12). Likes are the major determinant of aspirations and activities.

CAPACITY (13–14). Abilities are given more weight, and job requirements (including training) are considered.

2. *Exploration Stage* (Age 15–24)

Self-examination, role tryouts, and occupational exploration take place in school, leisure activities, and part-time work. Substages of the exploration stage are:

TENTATIVE (15–17). Needs, interests, capacities, values, and opportunities are all considered. Tentative choices are made and tried out in fantasy, discussion, courses, work, etc.

TRANSITION (18–21). Reality considerations are given more weight as the youth enters labor market or professional training and attempts to implement a self-concept.

TRIAL (22–24). A seemingly appropriate field having been located, a beginning job in it is found and is tried out as a life work.

3. *Establishment Stage* (Age 25–44)

Having found an appropriate field, effort is put forth to make a permanent place in it. There may be some trial early in this stage, with consequent shifting, but establishment may begin without trial, especially in the professions. Substages of the establishment stage are:

TRIAL (25–30). The field of work presumed to be suitable may prove unsatisfactory, resulting in one or two changes before the life work is found or before it becomes clear that the life work will be a succession of unrelated jobs.

STABILIZATION (31–44). As the career pattern becomes

---

* Donald Super, John Crites, Raymond Hummel, Helen Moser, Phoebe Overstreet, and Charles Warnath, *Vocational Development: A Framework for Research* (New York: Bureau of Publications, Teachers College, Columbia University, 1957), pp. 40–41.

clear, effort is put forth to stabilize, to make a secure place, in the world of work. For most persons these are the creative years.

4. *Maintenance Stage* (Age 45–64)

Having made a place in the world of work, the concern is now to hold it. Little new ground is broken, but there is continuation along established lines.

5. *Decline Stage* (Age 65 on)

As physical and mental powers decline, work activity changes and in due course ceases. New roles must be developed; first that of selective participant and then that of observer rather than participant. Substages of this stage are:

DECELERATION (65–70). Sometimes at the time of official retirement, sometimes late in the maintenance stage, the pace of work slackens, duties are shifted, or the nature of the work is changed to suit declining capacities. Many men find part-time jobs to replace their full-time occupations.

RETIREMENT (71 on). As with all the specified age limits, there are great variations from person to person. But, complete cessation of occupation comes for all in due course, to some easily and pleasantly, to others with difficulty and disappointment, and to some only with death.

---

himself in various adult roles, gratifying his needs in ways suggested to him by his encounters with work at home and in the wider world. Childhood is predominantly a fantasy stage.

ADOLESCENCE

Adolescence is, more than the other stages, an *exploratory* stage, in which the budding adult tries himself out more self-consciously and more realistically than he has before in various adult roles. At first this trial process is very *tentative,* for the child growing up does not yet know his aptitudes and his interests well, and he still knows little of adult roles, despite having played some of them as a child. He begins to think in terms of what interests him, he learns to take into account how well he succeeds in these activities, he recognizes that abilities are as important as interests, and he learns that society considers some goals to be more valid than others. His time perspective begins to lengthen. At age 14 the time of leaving college, seeking a job, or getting married seems remote, but at age 18 these future events and some that follow them (getting established in an occupation, having a home and children) begin to seem real: The adolescent learns, too, that interest, ability, values, and a sense of time are not enough: he learns that opportunity in the form of college or a suitable job, in the form of funds for education or capital for business, or in the form of a suitable mate is also important. Realism develops, in a period of rapid transition from a private to a public world.

Planning so that aspirations and opportunities may be more nearly congruent, so that abilities and interests may find outlets, becomes a valued characteristic and skill. Such planning has been called a compromising or synthesizing process, in which personal and social considerations are weighed and vocational decisions are made. These decisions are still exploratory at first: the decision is often simply to try something, be it a vocation, a job, or an evening's date. They later become somewhat more definitive. If the decisions are not reversed by negative experience, commitment to them increases with involvement and with the investment of time, money, and pride. This tendency for commitment to increase led Ginzberg (40) to call occupational choice an irreversible process. But he overstated the case, for Rothney (77), Flanagan and Cooley (34), Super (97), and others have shown that changes are frequent, not only in high school and college, but also during the first years of regular work experience. In the last-named study, only 16 percent of the twelfth graders had the same specific occupational preference as in ninth grade, and 56 percent had preferences that were in quite different occupational fields. At the age of 25, 22 percent were still floundering occupationally, while 37 percent had floundered in making most of their post–high school occupational decisions, frequently changing direction.

The increasing realism of vocational preferences and choices that Ginzberg postulated has, however, been confirmed by a number of studies. For example, physicians do tend to specify an occupational choice at age 18, and lawyers do tend to do so at about age 20. Sociologists point out that the difference in timing between physicians and lawyers is due to the organization of the educational and professional training systems, which require choices at those respective times. Some psychologists would add that individual differences also play a role: scientific interests mature in the early teens and social service interests considerably later. Some people are ready to specify choices earlier, and others are not ready until later. The notion of the irreversibility of choice has some validity, for the price of not deciding on medicine at the age of 18 or 19 and then making that choice later may be backtracking in college to take needed courses that were not included in the program chosen with a different objective.

YOUNG ADULTHOOD

The exploratory activity that characterizes adolescence continues until the middle twenties, at which time the trial process becomes less tentative. Commitment to an occupation (or to a husband and family) becomes more definite with the realism brought about by modified aspirations for using abilities and finding outlets for interests in a world that is now better understood. Stabilization in an occupation or a home sometime during the middle or late twenties is a frequently observed phenomenon, particularly in large-scale sociological analyses of work histories. This stage has therefore frequently been called the *establishment* stage, not only in describing occupational and career behavior, but also in analyzing family life and roles in the community.

MATURITY

The concept of establishment leads logically to that of *maintenance*, which implies that what has become, remains. That maintenance of what is established tends to be a feature of vocational life has been verified in America as well as in Europe, in studies by sociologists and psychologists. Exceptions are numerous, however, for some people who have once been established become disestablished as a result of illness, accident, war, or industrial change; and some continue to pioneer in new fields so that their careers involve a long-continuing establishment process. Even those who settle down in their "regular adult occupation" generally find that changing technology and changing economics force them to advance, to keep on mastering new subjects or skills, in order to stay in the same place. Thus, plumbers who have become heating specialists with the introduction of steam and hot-air heat find themselves obliged to become air-conditioning installation and maintenance men if they are to maintain a secure place in competition with other firms. Physicians, lawyers, and engineers also find that if they do not keep on learning they drop quickly behind their colleagues and their competitors. Women who take time out for several years of child rearing often need refresher training, many find new occupations as they prepare to rejoin the labor force, and some take advantage of their status to redirect their careers in new channels.

OLD AGE

After maturity comes old age. The *decline* of physical and mental capacities generally manifests itself little and slowly at first, but with increasing effect and rapidity as time goes on. At first it means deceleration: examples of such deceleration are tennis players who even in their thirties must learn to rely more on knowledge of the game and on skill than on speed and strength, physicians who learn to cut down their patient loads and to refer some of the more demanding cases, and auto mechanics who become service managers or gas-station attendants as their physical capacities decline.

Studies of attitudes toward work as men approach and enter retirement show that work and occupation do a great deal to structure life and to give it meaning and direction (35). For many, retirement therefore means loss of sense of purpose, loss of a routine that organizes life, loss of a role that gives one a recognized place in society. This sense of loss occurs whether the occupation is one in which self-expression and self-fulfillment are clearly possible, such as many professional and managerial positions, or whether the work is routine and intrinsically uninteresting. Both types of work organize the day's activity and involve certain expectations on the part of others: they thus constitute social roles. Being deprived of props such as these is a severe blow for many men and women who have worked all their lives. Nevertheless, those whose work continues into retirement and those who have developed significant non-"work" roles find retirement acceptable and even challenging. Scholars who continue to study and write in retirement and women who have chosen to be homemakers as well as workers are good examples of the latter.

The Developmental Tasks

Each age is characterized by a set of tasks that society expects persons of that age and sex to deal with effectively. Success in coping with the tasks of one age, Havighurst (47) theorized, is a prerequisite to dealing with those of the next age. Concerned with general adolescent development, he did not analyze in detail the vocational developmental tasks of adolescence or of adulthood.

Drawing on existing theory, since research was virtually lacking, the Career Pattern Study (98) identified the vocational developmental tasks of each stage and substage, together with the attitudes and behaviors associated with each. The vocational developmental tasks, the earliest encountered listed first, were conceived as:

> Crystallizing a vocational preference,
> Specifying it,
> Implementing it,
> Stabilizing in the chosen vocation,
> Consolidating one's status, and
> Advancing in the occupation.

The dozen or so attitudes and behaviors associated with the tasks can be illustrated by awareness of the need to crystallize (or specify, etc.) a vocational preference, by the use of resources such as counselors and summer jobs in carrying out a task, by awareness of factors to be considered, by awareness of the accidents or external events that might make acting on the preference difficult, and by acquiring more information concerning the preferred occupation.

The Career Pattern Study tested the adequacy of some of this theorizing. It analyzed the vocational maturity measures that it developed in studying behavior dealing with the task of crystallizing a vocational preference during the high school years. Information about the preferred occupation, including knowledge of the psycho-social conditions of work, about entry and advancement opportunities, and about the supply and demand of workers, increases with age and experience. Boys obtain work experience which involves more independence as they go through high school. Vocational preferences become more specific and are held with greater degrees of commitment as boys get older. Twelfth-grade boys consider alternatives, as ways of dealing with possible unforeseen events, more than do ninth-grade boys, even though ninth-grade boys typically express interest in a greater number of occupations than they do when in twelfth grade. All of these facts fit the picture of increasingly successful dealing with the early tasks of vocational development during high school.

Career Patterns

Progress through these life stages does not take place in a linear, uniform manner. Instead, some people reverse their occupational choices. Some who have become established are disestablished by internal or external developments. Some never do become established in a regular adult occupation; instead, their careers are unstable or involve many trials.

Important early work on career patterns was done by two sociologists (64). Their concept has since been used also by psychologists in the study of careers (96, 97, 43).

Miller and Form recognized that the concept of stages should not be applied rigidly; instead, they noted that careers can be typed in the same manner as life stages. Analysis of stability and change in careers showed that some people continue to change occupations or jobs throughout life, while others have periods of stability followed by new periods of trial, which in turn lead to stabilization for a second or third time. Thus, one can identify *stable* (direct entry into the life work), *conventional* (trial leading to stability), *unstable,* and *multiple-trial* careers. The processes that are dominant in the several life stages are now seen as processes that are repeated more than once throughout life, often in the sequence of exploration-establishment-maintenance-decline. The concept of processes in sequence has been used in a theory of *position* choice (104), in which each decision to occupy a position, whether that of worker, homemaker, or citizen, is viewed as involving exploration, establishment, maintenance and (in deciding to leave it) decline.

Socioeconomic Status

Men at each of the socioeconomic levels can be classified according to career patterns. Socioeconomic determinants do operate, for stable and conventional career patterns are more common at the higher socioeconomic levels, while multiple-trial and unstable patterns are more common at the lower levels.

The concept of life stages and the increased knowledge of career patterns raise a number of questions in vocational psychology that were not raised by differential psychology. Parental socioeconomic level is the starting point of the career pattern and one of its major determinants. That socioeconomic level is not the only determinant is, however, shown by the substantial numbers of persons whose careers are not what would have been predicted by the status of their parents. Intelligence, we have seen, is another determinant that is related to adult occupational status. There are other determinants of movement from position to position as the career unfolds. These determinants interact, modifying each other; for example, interest usually increases with success, provided the latter does not come too easily. The achievement of a given position at one point in the career influences movement toward and attainment of the next position.

The questions of change and mobility in terms of career patterns have only recently been the subjects of investigation by sociologists who pioneered in the study of careers, for the sociologists seem to have been interested primarily in the social causes of mobility. Similarly, economists have slighted these questions, for their interest in labor mobility has been only in the extent of movement and in its relationship to economic variables such as rates of pay and fringe benefits. Only recently, too, have these topics been investigated by psychologists, for most psychologists seem to have been unaware of the concept of careers and of the need to understand the psychological variables that affect their unfolding.

Race

The career development of racial minorities has not, until recently, been the subject of study by psychologists or sociologists. The acute awareness of discrimination in housing, education, and employment that developed during the 1960s did, however, bring minority issues out into the open and make it easier for behavioral and social scientists to study the career patterns and career determinants of minority groups.

Minority status has been shown to operate differently on different ethnic and religious groups: Orientals in North America tend to perform better in education and in work than their socially imposed handicap might lead one to expect. As a group, Jews similarly tend to achieve at higher levels than might be expected of them. Blacks, on the other hand, have until recently been depressed by discrimination rather than stimulated to overcome their social handicap.

Generalizations about career patterns that are helpful in dealing with members of majority groups need to be reexamined in dealing with members of minority groups. Racial or religious prejudice operates in the same way as do socioeconomic handicaps, spurring some people on to greater performance than might be predicted, deterring others from even trying, and preventing some who try from achieving.

Reverse discrimination, as in compensatory education and employment programs, may lead to achievement beyond what would have been accomplished without special outside help and thus helps counter the negative effects of prejudice.

Two issues are clearly central in the effects of race or other minority status on careers: the extent of the barrier to be overcome (discriminatory practices) and the motivation of the individual to overcome it. Barriers inhibit achievement; motivation may overcome them. When the barriers are widespread and impenetrable, as they have tended to be for blacks, motivation is destroyed. When they are not ubiquitous and insurmountable, as has been true for Orientals in North America, motivation may actually be increased.

Sex

The career patterns of men are better understood than are those of women, for they have been studied more thoroughly. Patterns are seen in women's careers, modified by the special impact on their employment of possible and actual marriage. High school and college girls are more likely than their brothers to aspire to short-term educational and training programs, reluctant to invest time and money in preparing for an occupation that may be only a stopgap situation. Often they are not helped to see that they are likely to reenter the labor market later in life, after ten or fifteen years of child-rearing. Their failure to recognize this likelihood is the result of a short time perspective which is characteristic of young people and of people from less economically advantaged homes. The jobs women get therefore tend to be merely time-filling, income-producing ways of keeping occupied instead of vocations in the real sense of this term.

Women who do have more highly developed vocational interests and motivation often find that their working lives are interrupted by the need to devote blocks of time to child-rearing, handicapped by homemaking responsibilities that demand more of them than of married men, or frustrated by discrimination against women in employment practices.

Their career patterns may therefore be characterized as *interrupted* or as *double-track* careers. The *conventional* career for women is still that of working and then devoting full time to homemaking, while the interrupted pattern of working, homemaking, and working again is increasingly common.

The Determinants of Career Patterns

The discussion of career patterns and of developmental tasks has brought out the fact that careers and career patterns are affected by a variety of economic, social, and psychological determinants. Table 7–2 depicts these determinants. Socioeconomic status, race, and sex make entry into educational and occupational positions easier or more difficult: the greater the resources a person has, the more informed people he can acquire information from, the fewer and lower the barriers of discrimination such as racial bias, the less he is handicapped by domestic responsibilities and by traditional barriers to the playing of certain roles, the greater the mobility of the individual and the more freedom he has to use his abilities and to develop and to express his interests.

TABLE 7–2. *Major determinants of career patterns.*

Psychological Determinants	Economic and General Determinants
Intelligence	Business Cycles
Special Aptitudes	Economic Booms and Depressions
Interests	Fads
Values	Technological Change
Needs	War
Social Determinants	Natural Disasters
Socioeconomic status	
Education	
Family Situation	
Military Service Obligation	
Citizenship	
Race	
Religion	
Sex	

Intelligence, special aptitudes, interests, values, and needs all operate in the same way. They affect career development just as, in Chapters 4 and 5, we saw that they affect occupational choice, success, stability, and satisfaction, for career development is a sequence of occupational choices and adjustments made in the course of a person's lifetime.

High socioeconomic status, intelligence, and education enable a person to know the importance of having good information in making decisions. A person's standing on these characteristics greatly influences his access to information, his ability to judge its quality, and his freedom to act upon conclusions drawn from it.

Interests, values, and special aptitudes guide people into certain channels rather than into others. Motivation determines how high a person aspires and how hard he works at acting upon his decisions. Intelligent, well-educated people who make good use of the resources that society makes available to them are more likely than are others to have stable or conventional career patterns and to pursue careers at the higher occupational levels. People who have less academic or special ability, obtain less adequate educations, and are less well-placed to make use of educational and occupational opportunities are more likely than others to have unstable or multiple-trial careers and to pursue them at lower occupational levels.

External career determinants in the form of business cycles, economic booms and depressions, fads, technological change, wars, and natural disasters such as earthquakes and floods are beyond the control of the individual. Wars destroy some industries and create others, changes in fashion make some occupations prosper as others decline, upsetting what had appeared to be stable careers and causing upward or downward mobility in individual careers. But internal factors also play a part: intelligence, education, and motivation to use good information well enable people to insure their careers in various ways, thus maximizing prospects of stability and minimizing losses due to accidents and to acts of God.

The Choosing Person

Internal and external determinants interact to produce decisions. The crucial question in career development is how internal and external determinants are synthesized to produce a decision.

Accident Theory

Accident theory, espoused by some sociologists, states that vocational development and occupational choice are largely accidents. In the context of this theory, the term *accident* denotes events or conditions beyond the control of the individual. The social class, ethnic group, and religious group into which one is born, for example, are not chosen by the person being born. One can, of course, change religion in adulthood, and one can identify and associate with another social class after achieving independence of the family, but freedom to alter even these is limited by the social environment, and people cannot change race. It is probably harder for most Catholics to change religion than it is for most Protestants, and harder for most Indians to change social class than it is for most Frenchmen. As for changing race, when that is defined in terms of color, the effect of the accident of birth is as nearly definitive as anything ever is.

Social class, family context, and the spheres of activity that these open and close to the individual are indeed potent determinants of career patterns and of occupational decisions. The view of occupational choice as largely accidental therefore appears at first to be unassailable.

We have seen, however, that aptitudes and motivation also play a part in career development. Although it is true that they are related to and affected by social class, there are still wide ranges of ability and of motivation within any one class. The correlation between the social status of the parents and the later occupation of the child is by no means perfect. Even the careers of identical twins reared in their own families are not identical, and those of fraternal twins and ordinary brothers or sisters are even less likely to be similar. It seems necessary to postulate a synthesizing role in the individual himself, to allow for a comparison of alternatives and a weighing of factors by a choosing person.

Self and Role Theories

Many psychologists have recognized that a person's actions are in part determined by his perceptions of himself, of the world, and of the situation in which he finds himself (56). However, the emphasis on the occupational model, on objective differential theory, which characterized vocational psychology until the 1950s, led to a neglect of person-centered theories in the study of vocational development.

SELF-ACTUALIZATION IN AN OCCUPATION

A self-concept theory of vocational development (92, 98) recognizes the importance of the formation of self-concepts, of their translation into occupational terms, and of their implementation as one becomes established in an appropriate occupation. If the whole life-span of an individual is considered, a series of self-concept modification and adjustment processes that follow in maturity are also important.

The formation process is one of exploration of the self and of the environment. It includes differentiation of the self from others, identification with others who can serve as models, and playing selected social (ethnic, familial, peer-group, educational and occupational) roles with a more or less conscious evaluation of the results, known as reality testing.

The translation of self-concepts into occupational terms takes place through one or more of three processes: identification, experience, and observation. Identification with an adult role model involves a global translation in which one says "I am like him" or "I want to be like him" without considering specific traits. Experience in a role in which one has been cast by circumstances provides many people with opportunity for the discovery of unsuspected vocational aspects of the self-concept; for example, a draftee assigned to service as a medical corpsman may discover unsuspected interests in and aptitudes for medicine. By observing, reading, and hearing things, one learns that some of one's aptitudes and interests are important in certain occupations.

The implementation process is one of action. The individual seeks and obtains the specialized education or training needed for the occupation to which he aspires, or he seeks and finds employment in it. Finding it, he *consolidates* his concept of himself as worker.

Modification takes place after entry and with establishment in the occupation, as encounters with the realities of the work call for further adjustments.

Preservation of the self-concept characterizes the maintenance stage, as the established person seeks to hold his own despite occupational change or the lessening of personal drive and energy. Further *adjustment* is called for during the years of decline as capacities and role expectations change more drastically.

The adequacy of the translation of self-concepts into occupational terms has been studied by people who hypothesize that the similarity of self-concepts and occupational concepts is greater for occupations in which one has expressed an interest than for those in which one has shown little interest. In one study (11), 135 twelfth-grade boys described their actual and ideal selves on a checklist. They also indicated which occupations, in a list scorable on Strong's Vocational Interest Blank, they were most and least interested in. A week later, each boy filled out the same adjective checklist to describe the typical member of his most and least preferred occupations. The self (both actual and ideal) and the most and least preferred occupations were then compared. As hypothesized, the boys' self-concepts were most like their concepts of members of their preferred occupations. The results of research such as this suggest that occupational choice is the result of perceived similarity of self and occupation, although they could mean that people attribute to their best-liked occupations the traits that they see in themselves. It seems likely that, in the average person, the numerous cues received concerning the characteristics of people in various occupations are more important than the less healthy mechanism of projection.

The implementation process has been examined in a series of studies of what has come to be known as the translation model. Hypothesizing that change of occupation is a function of the extent to which self- and occupational concepts agree, Bingham (10) administered a modification of Kelly's Role Construct Repertory Test to 82 full-time graduate students, all of them experienced classroom teachers beginning training to become school counselors. Testing was done at the beginning and end of the year of training. A control group consisted of 44 employed secondary school teachers with no guidance aspirations. Both groups rated themselves and the occupations of teacher and counselor, using traits shown by the Role Rep Test to have meaning for the respondent. Measures of agreement between self- and occupational descriptions were then derived.

The new counselors who had been teachers showed higher levels of incorporation of their self-concepts in the occupation of counselor than in that of teacher. That is, they attributed more of their own traits to the occupation to which they were changing than to the occupation that they were giving up. They made higher incorporation scores as counselors than did the teachers who served as controls. Contrary to expectation, the year of full-time professional preparation led to no increase in similarity of self- and counselor descriptions.

The preservation process was studied by Brophy (16). Methods similar to those later used by Blocher and Schutz were supplemented by job- and life-satisfaction questionnaires. His subjects were nurses employed in a New York hospital, who described the kind of person their jobs required them to be. Those whose self-concepts agreed with their view of their job requirements were better satisfied with their jobs than were those whose self- and job concepts were not similar. Cognitive dissonance theory, which postulates that people change their views of the external world to keep their self-concepts intact, might lead one to interpret these results as showing that occupationally dissatisfied nurses describe their jobs in incompatible terms in order to preserve their self-concepts. It requires fewer assumptions, however, to conclude that nurses who find that their jobs require them to act in uncongenial ways are dissatisfied with these jobs. It thus appears that occupational perceptions are determined more by external than by personal characteristics. In a situation requiring a choice, therefore, agreement of self- and occupational concepts does appear to determine vocational choice and adjustment.

Role theory makes an explicit attempt to take into account the external determinants of the occupational concepts that people hold. A role is a set of expectations that society, or some identifiable group in that society, has of people occupying a position. A person considering or pursuing an occupation finds that others have certain expectations of people who occupy positions such as his. His understanding of these expectations helps to shape his concept of the occupation.

The principal applications of role theory to vocational development have been in the study of role conflict and its resolution. Life-insurance salesmen, for example, are expected to be both altruistic ("Mr. Friendly") and materialistic ("million-dollar-a-year men"). Suffering discomfort from these conflicting value expectations, insurance salesmen tend to resolve them by suppressing the less firmly reinforced altruistic tendencies. Part of their occupational concept, and their related concepts, thus suffers (111). Air Force instructors suffer similarly from role conflict: regular officers with military career aspirations studied by Getzels and Guba (38) minimized the expectations associated with their instructor roles and played up the military, an acceptable solution in a military setting. Reserve officers aspiring to civilian futures, in contrast, remained dissatisfied and full of conflict because of personal altruistic values that were incompatible with the dominant authoritarian role of the military setting. Studies such as these have dealt only with people in a given occupation. It would be instructive to relate the perceived social role expectations of people in an occupation to the occupational concepts of persons seeking to enter that occupation, to study the changes that take place after entry into the occupation, and to ascertain the relationships between these changes and movement within or out of the occupation.

The choosing person who occupies a central place in the application of phenomenological and role theory to vocational development is generally a middle-class person: he is free to choose. Cultural anthropologists have made a distinction between expressive and responsive careers: the former are typical of the middle class and the latter typical of the upper and lower classes. *Expressive* careers are those in which people find outlets for their abilities and interests, in which the realization of self-concepts is possible, and which tend to be pursued because of the possibility of self-expression. *Responsive* careers are those in which the individual meets some demand of his environment, typically his family, choosing an occupation because his family expects him to, for status, or for survival.

Middle-class families in a modern economy do not typically have a substantial stake in a productive or distributive enterprise, for enterprise is corporate and their managerial or professional roles can be played in any of the enterprises. Their education, their skills, their mobility make freedom of choice a fact, and the only family pressures are thus to "make the most of one's opportunities."

Upper-class families do have substantial stakes in particular enterprises, although the corporate nature of industry and business make this stake more flexible now than formerly. Along with these vested interests go family traditions that make certain social roles seem quite appropriate and others very inappropriate: the scions of millionaires may become physicians or lawyers (the former less easily than a generation or two ago because of competitive admissions), but not ministers, social workers, YMCA secretaries, or schoolteachers. If not academically inclined, they are likely to become investment specialists or to enter politics at a fairly high level. They feel they must respond thus to the demands of their status.

Lower-class families, on the other hand, have limited resources and limited contacts. Their opportunities tend to be those of the nearby factory or shop, those that are open to people with limited education and no capital. These positions may offer little opportunity for self-expression, but they are sought because they provide an income and a place in the scheme of things.

Self-actualization, self-expression in the sense of finding outlets for the development of the best that is in one, is a need that characterizes persons who are free from environmental pressures. It appears to many to be an ideal for vocational development. It does postulate a choosing person who seeks to understand and to evaluate himself and his situation and to guide the unfolding of his career.

Summary

This chapter has outlined the principal life stages of growth, exploration, establishment, maintenance, and decline, relating them to career development and identifying the substages which are commonly observed. The patterning of careers typical of the various socioeconomic levels was described, with some discussion of the major internal (personal) and external (situational) determinants of these patterns. The developmental tasks that are typically encountered during the various stages of a career were identified, and those of adolescence—crystallizing, specifying, implementing, and stabilizing an occupational preference—were described in some detail.

The idea of a choosing person, one whose self-concept and whose understanding of the world around him guide his decisions as he seeks self-actualization, was developed in opposition to the emphasis put by accident theory on factors beyond the individual's control. Self-concepts are formed in early experiences with other people and with life situations; they are translated into occupational preferences through identification, experience, and observation. They are implemented in educational and occupational choices and modified by the resulting experiences. Situational determinants particularly relevant to the self are the role expectations of others, which are incorporated into the self-concept after modification by the individual's perception of them.

part four

Applications

Occupational psychology being the study of vocational development and of occupational choice, satisfaction, and success, its applications are to vocational guidance and counseling and to personnel selection and development. In Part IV, therefore, one chapter is devoted to personnel work and one to vocational guidance, insofar as these are psychological.

Selection and placement are viewed from two perspectives: the more traditional approach of matching men with jobs and the newer perspective, which views jobs as modifiable to suit men. Most research and most technological development have been of the former type, but manpower shortages and interest in the rehabilitation of the disabled and in the employment of the disadvantaged have led to the newer focus and to modified practices that draw on engineering psychology.

The several processes involved in the development and use of psychological methods of personnel selection are described, from the development of manning tables which show what types of employees are needed and when they are likely to be needed to the devising and validation of tests and other selection methods and instruments.

The development of the personnel resources of an enterprise is also treated. Topics covered include the analysis of lines of advancement, the analysis of replacement and expansion needs, the identification of talent that may be fostered on the job or in continuing education, and the development of programs for persons who are disadvantaged because of environment and early experience.

Vocational guidance and counseling are viewed first from a historical perspective, as a means of bringing out some of the differing emphases that are still seen in the field today, after two generations of vocational guidance services. Information concerning educational and occupational opportunities and requirements was the first major tool of vocational guidance, soon supplemented by psychological tests with normative and predictive data on education and occupations. Both kinds of data were then made more useful because of advances in methods of communicating with students and clients in personal counseling.

Evidence about the effectiveness of vocational counseling is also reviewed, for applied psychology has been characterized not only by its focus on practical problems, but also by its concern with evaluating the results of using the technology it develops for coping with them.

The problems with which vocational guidance deals and the places in which it deals with them are then surveyed. In conclusion, current trends are sketched, in an attempt to foresee what may be the emerging developments in the application of occupational psychology to vocational guidance.

chapter eight

Personnel
Selection and
Development

Personnel selection belongs to the more fundamental field of occupational psychology, for it draws on knowledge of the relationships between individual differences and occupational success. It uses the methods and instruments developed for the study of psychological characteristics and their bearing on occupational outcomes. As an applied field, it has developed a significant methodology and considerable stature of its own. Therefore, a whole volume in this series is devoted to personnel selection (25), and the reader interested in a more detailed treatment will wish to consult that volume. One section of this chapter consists of a brief survey of personnel-selection principles and methods, and the rest deals with personnel development after initial selection and placement. The latter emphasis befits the broadened, if unorthodox, definition of occupational psychology, which takes career development into account.

Selection and Placement

The first two parts of this book have shown how individual differences are related to occupations, how they are measured, and how occupational ability and motivation patterns have been established by research. The fact that men and jobs can be matched is one of which industry and government have made much use in their efforts to enhance the value to individuals of employment and to increase worker efficiency.

The task of developing company norms for personnel selection and placement is considerably easier than that of developing standards for more general vocational guidance or manpower planning. One reason for the difference is that jobs vary less from position to position, from department to department, and from branch to branch in one company than they do from one company to another. Another is that a company seeking to develop a test or other selection procedures for its own use has stronger claims on the time of applicants, employees, and supervisors than does an outsider coming to collect test and performance data for some outside project. The greater the similarity of manufacturing or business processes and products, and the more immediate the common management, the greater the similarity of personnel needs, job specifications, selection standards, work methods, and job performance. The greater the stake of the company in the effective selection of personnel, the more willing it is to devote the resources necessary to the development and collection of data for predicting success and for evaluating performance. The result of the greater ease in developing company tests and norms has been more personnel-selection research in corporations and in certain government agencies than in the public employment services.

The matching of men and jobs, as Dunnette (25) has pointed out, may have as its objective the best possible match for the man himself, to provide him with the best opportunities to use his aptitudes and abilities and to find outlets for his interests. Or it may seek the best match for the company, in order to meet company manpower needs efficiently.

One of the clearest illustrations of the conflict between these two objectives came to light in the classification of aviation cadets for aircrew training during World War II. Men who qualified for both pilot and navigator training were sent, sometimes to one, sometimes to the other type of training, depending upon the momentary needs and quotas of the respective training schools. At times men who qualified for and preferred the pilot training were sent to navigation training because they were qualified and needed there, and at other times men who qualified for and preferred the navigation training were sent to pilot training because they were qualified and needed in that specialty.

Such incidents are more likely to happen, of course, in time of crisis than in normal times and under permissive conditions. In normal times, most jobs are filled by people with both the needed qualifications and the desire to do that kind of work. The expectation is that others who are less qualified or who have different objectives will seek and find other more appropriate outlets.

For some demanding positions that are not easily filled, a compromise is usually sought, in which the individual selected will find opportunities for the use of his abilities and for the expression of his interests, and the organization will acquire the manpower needed to carry out its functions. One way of making such a compromise is to modify the job to suit the individual who seems best suited and available.

Problems of the adaptation of jobs to men, rather than of the selection of men for jobs, are faced most often in cases of a person already in the employment of a company who is no longer needed in or able to perform the duties of his former positions. For him some new placement should, in fairness, be found. It is more difficult to turn the person in question away on the ground that there are no suitable openings, for such an employee has built up moral equity in the company, and the company has an investment in and a debt to him. In cases involving the physically handicapped, for example, job modification to suit individual capacities has become a widely accepted practice, aided by developments in engineering psychology.

Selection Processes

There are four steps in the development of a selection and placement program: Setting up manning tables, job analysis, man analysis, and instrument development and validation. Each of these is considered in the paragraphs that follow.

Manning Tables

Before the actual work of personnel selection can get under way, decisions must be made about the kinds and numbers of persons to employ. The organization must have a manning table, a chart indicating what kinds of jobs are needed in order to accomplish its work and how many positions of each type must be filled. For this table to be developed, the production, distribution, and service objectives and functions must be identified, and the manpower needed in order to attain them must be determined. These objectives and functions are problems of production management, office management, sales management, and the like; personnel management and personnel psychology are involved when functions and tasks are to be translated into positions and therefore into personnel requirements. There is some tendency for decisions to be made on the basis of tradition, precedent serving as a too convenient rule of thumb. But personnel psychology, by bringing to bear on these problems the methods of job analysis that it shares with industrial engineering and the methods of man analysis that are peculiarly its own, has made significant contributions to the improvement of manning tables.

Its contributions have been particularly significant when new processes and new equipment have created enterprises that lack traditions to guide practice, as in the space agencies. The contributions sometimes consist of ascertaining ways in which the flow of work can be organized to require fewer persons, or persons with lower levels of training, than those originally needed or planned on. Positions calling for skills that are in short supply can sometimes be broken down into less skilled components; for the less skilled tasks, workers can be trained in brief and intensive programs. Positions that do not attract and hold employees can be studied and restructured to make them more attractive to persons of the calibre needed. The handling of certain engineering functions by technicians has thus, in many places, freed professionally trained men from tasks that to them were routine and lacking in challenge, but that to less intellectually inclined workers were very satisfying. Similar trends are observable in the health services, in education, and in other fields, although the impetus more often arises from financial or manpower shortages than from rational or scientific analysis. Solutions are more often found by common sense than by the psychological study of the job and of those performing it.

However they may be arrived at, manning tables do give an organization a picture of the types and numbers of personnel that it appears to need in order to do the work necessary to attain its objectives.

Job Analysis

A list of job titles does not convey enough to managers or to employment interviewers to make possible the recruitment and hiring of the needed personnel. Job specifications are needed to define what the worker does and to identify what knowledge and skills he must have. The latter may be summed up briefly in terms of a license, a professional degree, or previous job experience. But, if selection procedures are to be developed that will help to identify qualified people with unorthodox training or experience, the content as well as the symbols of the knowledge and skill must be specified. For example, when the New York City subway system revamped its signal system many years ago, the need for experts with railroad-signal experience led to the identification of an unemployed printer who handled the job of subway-signal expert very well. He had developed the needed knowledge as a model-railroad enthusiast, and this *knowledge* had been described on the job order. One could not have known that this hobby would qualify a person as a subway-signal expert without awareness of just what a person must know in order to handle both tasks.

Job-analysis methods have been developed by psychologists for occupational analysis and description (81, 30). These methods provide data that aid in placement and in test construction. They are used by vocational educators for curriculum development, by industrial engineers for planning work layouts and production methods, and by various specialists for salary and wage setting. The specific content sought in the job analysis and included in the description varies somewhat with the purpose of the job description. In *job descriptions* for use in the state employment services, for example, the common elements of jobs in various companies are stressed, but the *specifications for a position* to be filled in a particular company are specific to that company and even to one of its departments. When the purpose is to develop a battery of selection tests, the focus is on activities that reveal the differentiating aptitudes and other traits needed to master the occupation or to perform the work of the job. In wage setting, however, the stress is on duties that help fix the level of training needed and of responsibility assigned.

The methods of job analysis consist of securing descriptions of duties and methods from those who do the work, either orally or in writing; securing logs of daily activities from workers; observing them at work; talking with them about the work; and doing the work oneself. Critical incidents, consisting of something a worker has done that was particularly good or successful, or something that was particularly bad or unsatisfactory, together with discussions of what was good or bad about it, have proved helpful in ascertaining traits that should be sought in selecting airline pilots and people for other especially demanding work.

The *Dictionary of Occupational Titles*, which defines jobs in terms of duties and tasks performed as revealed in interviews and questionnaires, is a good source of ideas about the kinds of aptitudes and interests that contribute to success in the jobs described.

For example, the job of *Medical Technologist* is defined as follows:

> Performs chemical, microscopic, and bacteriologic tests to provide data for use in treatment and diagnosis of disease: Receives specimens from laboratory, or obtains such body materials as urine, blood, pus, and tissue directly from patient, and makes quantitative and qualitative chemical analyses (BIOCHEMISTRY TECHNOLOGIST). Cultivates, isolates, and identifies pathogenic bacteria, parasites, and other micro-organisms (MICROBIOLOGY TECHNOLOGIST). Cuts, stains, and mounts tissue sections for study by PATHOLOGIST. Performs blood tests and transfusions, studies morphology of blood, and prepares vaccines and serums. Groups or types blood and crossmatches that of donor and recipient to ascertain compatibility. Determines basal metabolism rate. Engages in medical research to further control and cure disease. May calibrate and use equipment designed to measure glandular and other bodily activity (RADIOISOTOPE TECHNOLOGIST). May take electrocardiograms. May train and supervise MEDICAL-LABORATORY ASSISTANT and student TECHNOLOGISTS (MEDICAL TECHNOLOGIST, TEACHING SUPERVISOR).

Study of this material and of supporting test data led job analysts in the United States Employment Service to describe the characteristics of workers in this job as follows:

> Physical demands are light, involving reading, handling, and seeing and making visual (color) discrimination and accommodation while sitting or standing for some time; work is indoors; involves applying principles and knowledge to define problems, collect data, establish facts, and draw conclusions. Requires two to four years of training.

The General Aptitude Test Battery, administered to 113 medical-technology students whose work was rated by their supervisors, showed that they did indeed possess significant amounts of certain specific aptitudes. Their *Occupational Aptitude Pattern* included scores at least as high as the cutoff scores indicated on these four aptitudes:

| General Intelligence: | 110 | Form Perception: | 105 |
| Verbal Aptitude: | 110 | Clerical Perception: | 110 |

Man Analysis

The distinction between job and man analysis is frequently blurred, because the analysis of a job typically involves studying the people who do the job. Logically and methodologically, however, the two kinds of analysis are distinct activities. As the term implies, the focus in job analysis is on the *job:* on what procedures are used to attain what objectives with what materials, what data, or what people. In man analysis, on the other hand, the focus is on the *man:* what he knows, what skills he has acquired in training, what aptitudes and personality traits he brings with him to the training or to the entire job. In job analysis, the assumption is that one can infer knowledge, skills, aptitudes, and personality from the tasks performed. In man analysis, the assumption is that one must have the knowledge, skills, aptitude, and personality traits of successful workers in order to succeed in that work. The two methods are of course complementary, and neither is sufficient by itself. In practice, job analysts with a psychological orientation tend to start with the man doing the work.

The methods of man analysis include the interview, application forms and personnel records, and tests. These provide data that can show the differentiating characteristics of persons who succeed in varying degrees in the job or occupation in question—if, that is, suitable criteria of success are available.

Instrument Development and Validation

Interviews, forms, and tests, however, are not solely methods of obtaining data for the description of successful and unsuccessful workers. They are also selection and classification instruments, which, if validated, are helpful in identifying potentially successful employees.

It should be emphasized that it is not just *tests* that are developed, tried out, and validated for personnel selection. The same stringent standards can and must be applied to *interviews*, to *application blanks*, to *letters of recommendation*, and to any other procedure or instrument that yields data used in making personnel decisions.

Studying interviews is rather more difficult than is studying tests. Test materials are easily accessible, for answers are recorded on answer sheets in brief and manageable form. Test scores are not threatening to experimenters, for rarely does a reputation stand or fall on a test that is being tried out. Interview materials are more difficult to examine, for interviews must be recorded, transcribed, and analyzed by laborious methods even when a computer does the analysis. Furthermore, interview research is often threatening to the staff members using interviews, for to have conducted a poor interview is likely to be seen as evidence that one is a poor human being.

The first step in instrument development is to decide, on the basis of job and man analysis, *what data are to be obtained*, and, on the basis of knowledge of prior work with various methods and instruments, *how they may best be obtained*. An application blank, a guide to employment interviewing, a test or battery of tests and inventories may already have been devised and tried out with subjects like those with whom one is to work. It is likely, however, that there will be some situational differences that require trying out the instruments in the new setting. It has been found, for example, that tests that were useful for selecting department-store sales clerks in Minneapolis did not differentiate good from poor sales clerks in a New York department store. In another situation, dexterity tests that correlated positively with production under one set of conditions correlated negatively, with the same criterion and for the same workers, under changed circumstances. An interest inventory that differentiated successful from unsuccessful life-insurance salesmen in one company at one time did not make any such distinction at another time when labor-market conditions were different.

There is, therefore, a certain amount of risk involved in assuming that what worked well at one time, in one place, will work at another time or in another place. The standard methods of test construction should be used, whether an instrument or method is adopted without change or a new one is to be developed. The reliability of the instrument or method (the degree to which it agrees with itself when one half is compared to the other half or when it is used again with the same subjects after a reasonable interval of time) and its validity (its ability to differentiate between successes and failures) need to be studied.

The second step in instrument development, *establishing the validity of the instrument,* is by no means simple. To know whether or not an interview procedure or a test predicts success in a job, one must have an operational definition of *success in that job* and a reliable measure of that kind of success. Agreement on definitions is difficult to achieve, and reliable data are difficult to obtain. For example, success in selling seems at first to be easily scaled on the basis of the dollar volume of sales, but such data are deceptive if the sales territories involved differ in the per capita wealth of their inhabitants or in the density of their population. Furthermore, the man who sells a great deal unscrupulously during his first year may have fewer repeat sales in his second year than does the man who sells less at first but responds to long-term consumer needs and maintains his sales over a period of years. Assembly-line workers tend to produce amounts that are close to, but not above, a group-approved norm: if they produce more, they are ostracized as "rate-busters." Supervisors' ratings of employees are pertinent indications of success, for they affect raises and promotions, but ratings have often been shown to be affected by irrelevant considerations such as friendship.

The personnel psychologist is therefore usually forced to settle for some criterion, or combination of criteria, of success that reflects reasonably well the employer's ideas of what constitutes success in that job. The psychologist seeks to make the criterion as reliable as possible.

Once a selection instrument or method has been chosen or devised, and once a criterion of success has been settled on, *the third step* is to *use the instrument* with a group of candidates for employment. It is desirable to analyze separately those who have relevant experience and those who lack such experience. It is then important to abstain from using these data in making employment decisions, so that later one may take *the fourth step* and *ascertain the relationship between selection instrument data* (e.g., answers to application-blank questions, interviewers' ratings, or test scores) *and success data* (e.g., supervisors' ratings or sales volume). *Finally, a cutting score is set* that is high enough to reject probable failures but low enough to avoid turning down too many probable successes. If the test uses new items or a new scoring procedure, the study is then replicated on a second group to eliminate the possibility that the first results were caused by chance.

The methods of test construction and validation have been the subject of many books (100, 59, 86), and the literature of personnel psychology is full of studies of the validity of selection methods (95, 39). However, there is no universally applicable battery of questionnaires and tests, no "package" ready for use in any new situation without further study. Nor is such a kit likely to become available in the foreseeable future.

Many new questions have arisen during the past few years, questions of the applicability of currently standardized instruments and methods to disadvantaged persons and questions of the propriety of asking certain kinds of questions for employment purposes. In the former category is the question of what kinds of measures will assess the prospects of success that would result if a disadvantaged person is given the opportunity to move in a culture that is different in significant ways from the one he has known. In the latter category is the question of whether an employer can legitimately inquire into the personal life of a prospective employee: drinking habits or marital happiness may affect the quality of his work, but should the employer limit his inquiries to success in training for and experience in the type of work in question? These are only two examples of the many unresolved issues in the use of selection methods.

The considerable amount of work done so far, however, has led to the improvement of interviewing methods, the devising of better application blanks, the development and refinement of tests and inventories for the measurement of a variety of aptitudes and traits, and the demonstrations of their validity in many different types of selection situations.

One study of the contribution of a test battery to improved selection serves as a model, because of its thoroughness in the work of test construction, its good design, the large number of its subjects, and the relevance of its criterion (30). Early in World War II, some 1300 applicants were assigned to flying training regardless of their scores on the selection tests. The test data were set aside and kept confidential until the men had finished training. In this sample of non-test-selected young men, the failure rate in flying training was 50 percent (one failure for each success), whereas experience showed that the failure rate would have been only 25 or 30 percent had the tests been used in selection. The failure rate was thus cut in half by the use of empirically developed tests.

Personnel Development

When manning tables are filled in with the ages of the people occupying each position and with data on the tenure typical of each type of position, it immediately becomes evident that some places will soon become open through retirement. Other positions, although it is not so evident, will also become open because of advancement, resignation, or expansion.

Management Succession

The term "management succession" has come into use to denote the preparation of younger replacements ready to take the places of older men who advance or retire or whose positions need to be duplicated because of expansion. The identification of men and women in a manning table who are likely to move, for whatever reasons, points out the vacuums that may be created in the organization and raises questions of replacement or of succession. Three questions then arise: Where will the replacements come from, how will they be identified, and how will they be made ready for their forthcoming responsibilities?

Career Ladders

The answer to the *replacement* question is provided by the development of career ladders. One way of developing a career ladder is to plot, on a manning table, the origins of each of the persons currently filling a position. Some of these origins will prove to be in the organization itself, as men or women have advanced from less responsible to more responsible positions as in Figure 8–1. At some point, each person has come into the organization from outside, whether from a position in another company or from a training institution: these origins, too, can be plotted.

The career ladder shows where people have come from. There is a danger in relying exclusively on this method, for some of the origins may be nonexistent or obsolete by the time the career

PHOTOMAPPING CAREER FIELD

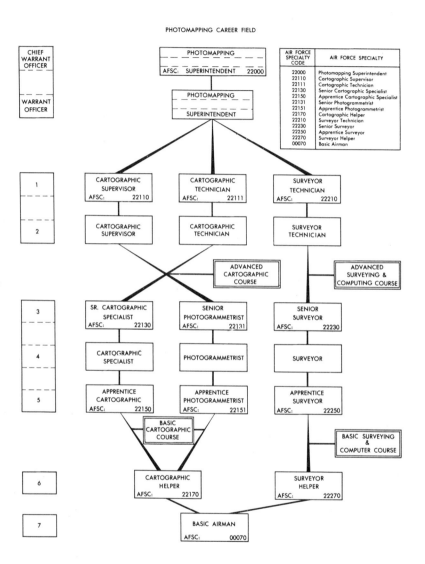

FIGURE 8–1. *Diagram of Air Force Career Ladder: Photomapping. Carroll L. Shartle, Occupational Information (2nd ed.) (Englewood Cliffs, N.J.: Prentice-Hall, 1959), p. 232.*

ladder is drawn. Efforts must therefore be made to go beyond experience and make informed guesses concerning future sources of supply for each position, whether it is an entry job or an advancement job. Such efforts are problems of industrial ecology, of occupational sociology, and of personnel administration, rather than of personnel psychology. But the data provided by work in these fields are essential to the analysis of the psychological dynamics of career development.

Career Assessment

The task of *identifying* persons who may be qualified to assume greater responsibility in an organization involves psychological variables and is within the realm of personnel psychology. The task of providing experiences that will enable employees to be ready to assume such responsibilities involves psychoeducational procedures, with which personnel psychology is also equipped to deal.

The identification of talent within an organization takes place in a variety of ways. Some of these are a part of routine personnel work. In well-developed personnel programs, regular performance appraisals record the evaluation of an employee's work. These appraisals are based on a supervisor's analysis of the subordinate's performance and of his personal and professional growth and on discussions of goals and their attainment during the year past and during the year ahead. These analyses and discussions give perspective on the problems, achievements, growth, and development of the employee and clues as to the directions and extent of probable future growth. Other methods of identifying talent involve special assessments of promising personnel by members of a special unit in the corporation or by consultants brought in for the purpose of identifying talent. A few large corporations maintain a staff of psychologists for this purpose, while many others use the services of consulting organizations whose main function is the identification of talent.

Although some effort has been expended on the identification of persons holding lower-level jobs whose abilities might be developed for middle- and higher-level positions, until recently most effort has gone into the identification of talent from outside the organization for middle- and higher-level positions. Here the immediate stakes are clearly great. The methods used involve clinical interviews, high-level verbal-aptitude tests such as Terman's *Concept Mastery Test,* or creativity test batteries such as Guilford's. Murray's *Thematic Appercep-*

tion Test provides the psychologist with a set of stories that may be analyzed in order to reveal recurring themes or trends. These trends are presumed (and have sometimes been shown) to be related to behavior in real-life situations. Despite the serious work of researchers such as J. P. Guilford, Calvin Taylor, William Henry, and others interested in creativity, there is still little to be reported in the way of sound applications of psychology to executive selection. Such applications are lacking partly because much of the scientific work is still confined to the psychological laboratory. The development of tests, such as those of divergent or creative rather than convergent or conformist thinking, and the factor analysis of aptitudes are prime examples of laboratory work not yet widely applied. One reason they are not applied is that those who work with candidates for high-level jobs in industry deal with numbers of subjects that are too small to permit the validation and cross-validation of predictor measures against satisfactory criteria of performance. For example, a large corporation selects a president only once in several years, and the data on the man selected cannot be pooled with data on the selection of presidents for other corporations, because the criterion situations arc quite different. As a result of such problems, most current work on executive identification is "clinical": it is subjective and dependent on hunches rather than on objective evidence. Although it may seem very plausible, it may be invalid. Whether research has been objective or subjective, practice depends primarily upon the unvalidated wisdom and insights of clinicians, whose principal claims to expertise are training and specialization in executive selection rather than demonstrable effectiveness.

Identifying and developing the latent talents of the disadvantaged has, during the past few years, been the object of renewed interest (58). Such talents had, it should be noted, been the subject of study nearly forty years ago in an earlier period of discovery of the poor, the unemployed, and the unassimilated (72, 73). That abilities and motivations are the result of interaction between the individual and his environment and that a limited environment means limited interaction, limited ability, and limited motivation have finally become clear to most psychologists and to most educators. It has now been realized that methods of assessing talents in persons who have been exposed to a varied and stimulating subculture may well not be appropriate for persons who have been exposed only to a more limited, less stimulating, and even stultifying subculture. It has been shown, for example, that disadvantaged children are less handicapped as very young children, before their environment has had much time to affect them, than they are after several years of living in deprived homes and attending substandard schools. It is for this reason that books have appeared with titles such as *Death in an Urban Classroom.*

Career Development

Efforts are now being directed toward the development of hitherto underdeveloped talents, not only in very young children and in high school and college students, but also in business and industry through programs of compensatory education and training.

Continuing education for the development of talent has, then, become the main focus of work both with the disadvantaged and with the advantaged. Continuing education is relevant for the unemployed and untrained, for semiskilled and skilled workers faced with technological change, for clerical workers displaced by automated record keeping, for professional men overwhelmed by the knowledge explosion, and for managers or owners who must coordinate skills and make use of specialized knowledge. Although these are primarily problems of pedagogy, of educational rather than of personnel psychology, the personnel psychologist needs to be aware of their nature and of the means available for their solution. He is likely to be involved in the development of solutions and in the evaluation of their effectiveness. Education, as has frequently been pointed out, is as much a function of modern business and industry as it is of schools, and personnel psychology must embrace educational psychology as much as it does psychometrics, occupational psychology, and social psychology.

Four levels of employee development activity can be identified. *The first* is that of the teaching of basic *skills in communication* (reading, writing, and speaking English) and in computation (arithmetic and some algebra). These skills are the essence of compensatory education. Programs such as those of the Job Corps have of necessity found ways of making such education meaningful to school dropouts, engaging them in activities that they wanted to pursue and in which they found they needed to learn to read, to write, or to calculate.

The second level of employee development activity is that of teaching *specialized skills or knowledge* needed in a particular job. These are represented not just by elementary tool courses such as television maintenance and repair or machine bookkeeping, but by related basic courses in physics or in accounting and programming. These related courses are designed to make persons who might otherwise remain static in obsolescent jobs more versatile and more upwardly mobile.

The third level is that of the teaching of *advances in theory and in related methodology* in the higher-level occupations, as in the study of physics by biologists moving into the developing field of biophysics and in the study of political science or sociology by lawyers concerned with the emerging problems of a rapidly evolving democracy.

The fourth and final level is that of the broad *cultural education* of top management personnel. The provision of a summer or a semester of study of the liberal arts for corporation executives whose background is strictly in engineering is an example. Just what the occupation or economic gains are is uncertain, but such programs have been popular because of the hope that a more broadly educated executive would develop greater ability to see emerging organizational and social problems and greater ability to mobilize relevant talents for their solution.

Summary

One of the major applications of occupational psychology is in the selection and placement of personnel. Selection and placement involve a variety of procedures. Manning tables show the number and types of personnel needed. Job and man analysis provide information about needed skills and traits. Tests and other methods needed to identify persons capable of meeting organizational needs are supplied by instrument development and validation. The processes of personnel or career development include management or the planning of executive advancement, the analysis and use of career ladders for the guidance of employees and for the identification of talent, and the planning and conduct of programs for personnel development. The problems of employing and training the disadvantaged and of selecting top management have been considered in these connections. In the case of the disadvantaged, handicaps in education usually result in handicaps on tests and in training as hitherto conducted, making success in practical work situations difficult to predict. In the case of top executives, the numbers available for study in any one situation make the validation of selection instruments difficult. Psychology, sociology, and education have much to contribute to the theory and practice of personnel administration.

chapter nine

Vocational
Guidance
and Counseling

The application of occupational psychological knowledge has taken place primarily in two areas: personnel selection and placement, which was discussed in Chapter 8, and vocational counseling, which will be discussed in detail in this chapter. Personnel selection and placement are processes usually viewed from the perspective of the organization that they are designed to serve. The worker is chosen and the jobs are organized by a corporation that has impersonal aims. The process of counseling, on the other hand, is seen primarily from the perspective of the individual who is making decisions about his own destiny. The individual wants to act in ways that will be the most rewarding for him personally and professionally.

Some Background on Vocational Counseling and Guidance

The idea that some men might be better than others at doing specific jobs is not a modern invention. The Roman statesman Cicero wrote of differential talents for different jobs and different suitability of people for various occupations. Before him, Plato, in his discussion of the perfect city, wrote of matching men and jobs in the Greek ideal.

Historically, the idea of freedom of occupational choice is comparatively new. In ancient and medieval times, a person had little freedom to choose an occupation that appealed to him. Social and occupational level and even field were determined primarily by birth.

A son did what his father had done or was apprenticed to someone at the same level; a daughter married into another family in the same social circle as her own. With the Renaissance and Reformation came increased recognition of the fundamental humanity, capacity, and uniqueness of the individual. Each man was the center of a universe of his own construing as well as a member of a general human society. With the Enlightenment came a broadening of the humanist approach to individual destiny and the application of that approach to politics and economics.

Finally, with the coming of democracy in industrial society, came the relative freedom of choice of occupations. In the implementation of the freedom of choice enjoyed by contemporary youth, vocational counseling came into its own.

Vocational guidance, at one time defined as the process whereby the individual is helped "to choose, prepare for, enter upon, and progress in the occupation" (68), traces its modern history in the U.S. to Frank Parsons of Boston and in Europe to A. G. Christiaens of Brussels. In his classic 1909 work, *Choosing a Vocation*, which was concerned with the floundering of young people as they leave school, Parsons outlined the three steps crucial in helping young men to select an appropriate occupation: (1) analyzing the man—that is, the person gaining understanding about himself and his counselor gaining understanding about him; (2) studying occupations—that is, understanding the demands and rewards of the occupation; and (3) counseling the man about the occupation—that is, relating the demands of the occupation to the characteristics of the man in a process quaintly referred to by Parsons as "true reasoning."

Information in Vocational Guidance

As vocational-guidance services were first being developed, methods of assessing individual abilities were still in the laboratory stage, counseling methods were not yet being subjected to scientific study, and information about educational and occupational opportunities and demands was still little more than hearsay. Collecting and systematizing information about colleges, trade schools, and occupations was, however, relatively easy and required no technology. The result was that early efforts at vocational guidance depended largely on the supply of information about opportunities to youth, information that was collected by talking with people and that was written up in more or less literary form.

In due course, economists, sociologists, and psychologists became interested in systematizing the collection and analysis of information concerning education and occupations. Job-analysis methods were devised by psychologists like Morris Viteles to show the estimated aptitude requirements of various jobs. Later, as tests were being applied to the study of occupations in the pioneer work at the University of Minnesota during the depression of the 1930s, job analysis became more objective. It led the U.S. Employment Service to develop the *Dictionary of Occupational Titles* with its classified occupational descriptions and its estimates of worker traits. At the same time, economists developed methods for studying occupational trends, and the Bureau of Labor Statistics started publishing the *Occupational Outlook Handbook* and a related quarterly.

Educational information was also being analyzed in more penetrating ways during the years preceding and following World War II. College directories published data on types of educational opportunities and resources, and, during the 1950s, studies began to appear that reported on the psychological characteristics of colleges and universities. Robert Knapp, Robert Pace, Alexander Astin, and others showed that colleges differ in the kinds of students they attract and the kind they produce. Studies by such people make available the data on higher education that enable a prospective student to choose more intelligently the kinds of influences to which he will be subjected in college.

Studies of decision making, of programmed instruction, and of the use of information in decision making have helped to restore the information process and services from a somewhat lowly, if essential, place in vocational guidance to a more respected place. It is now recognized that the collection, analysis, and provision of useful information in a usable way is a technology in its own right (12), and those who are skilled in this technology are very much in demand for the development of audio-visual aids and of computer systems for information processing and display in educational and vocational guidance.

Testing as Part of Vocational Guidance

Although the matching of men and jobs has provided the basic framework of vocational guidance from the 1930s until recent years, the role of psychological testing in this process has varied. During World War I, Army personnel psychologists developed tests of ability that were useful in large-scale military placement on the basis of intelligence.

The 1920s saw an increase in civilian testing and its applications. During the 1930s, unemployment forced men to review their aptitudes and occupational outlets under circumstances in which choice was often limited: many men would have been glad to accept any kind of employment, and therefore they sought counseling on redirecting their efforts. It was in this period that the landmark Minnesota Studies of Mechanical Aptitude were put to use by the Employment Stabilization Research Institute, in an attempt to understand the characteristics important in obtaining and holding jobs in such times.

World War II brought with it new problems of matching men and jobs, and, in a time when maximum efficiency in the use of manpower became exceedingly critical, military psychologists once again set the pace for the development of instruments for selection and placement according to aptitudes, interests, and personality. Following World War II, many men and women needed help in making the transition back to civilian employment, and the individual problems of occupational choice were seen as part of the nation's readjustment to a peacetime economy. As noted earlier in this book, since World War II, advances in psychological testing of particular importance to occupational planning have been made in the use of multifactor aptitude measures.

An influence on vocational guidance that has been concerned with, but not limited to, testing has been the program of the Veterans Administration. In response to the need to assist millions of returning servicemen, the Veterans Administration established vocational counseling services in its own offices and hospitals and on college campuses. The centers established on campuses were the forerunners of many of today's college counseling centers. The vocational counseling practices and standards of the Veterans Administration set many precedents, having a lasting effect on vocational counseling and on the psychological specialty of counseling psychology. The effects of this program and its successors are clearly seen in the Greyston Conference (99), which assessed the history, the present status, and the future of the specialty of counseling psychology.

Counseling as Part of Vocational Guidance

The counseling philosophy of the late Victorian pioneers in vocational guidance relied on a rational attitude in the counselee in the selection of an occupation. A development in psychology that changed this philosophy and was a major influence on vocational counseling, although only after World War I, was the mental health movement. This movement began at the turn of the century in mental hospitals, most of whose inmates had been unable to adjust to life without distortions of reality, and was greatly modified with the spread of psychoanalytic theory after World War I. Later still, early in World War II, the psychologist Carl Rogers proposed that disturbed individuals should experience an atmosphere of acceptance, in which they could come to accept themselves and so see themselves more accurately. This nondirective, or client-centered, approach made vocational counselors more aware of how their clients saw things and gave the counselors methods for dealing with irrational but very real attitudes.

With the incorporation of nondirective counseling approaches and methods into much of vocational counseling, the place of testing in the counseling process was reconsidered and modified. Vocational counseling had historically relied on tests and other such information, on appraisal and on assessment, as a major part of the counseling process. In nondirective counseling, tests were not called for as tools for a counselor's use in diagnosis or prognosis. Rather, testing, like educational and occupational information, became a resource for use in a collaborative search for information relevant to a question. The selection of the tests to be given was seen as a decision that required the active cooperation and informed participation of the client using the counselor as a consultant. This view made the counseling a more truly interactive situation, with more responsibility placed on the client as the ultimate decision maker. \

Vocational counseling today, then, is the result of a number of movements that had their formal beginnings in efforts to assist young men in selecting appropriate occupations. Educational and occupational information has been collected and organized to make this helping process more effective, and advances in psychological testing have been systematically exploited. More recently, vocational guidance and counseling have incorporated understandings from the field of mental health, producing an approach to human development that involves adjustment to work as a central aspect of a person's total life pattern.

Evidence for the Effectiveness of Counseling

Any discipline that aspires to be scientific must periodically look at how well it is doing. In this case the question is: What difference does counseling make? Are men and women who have sought professional counseling better off or worse off, on the average, than their uncounseled peers? It used to be thought that if counseling did not help, at least it would not make a person worse. Recent evidence on this question has made even this simple statement suspect. What is the evidence for the effectiveness of counseling?

CAMPBELL'S TWENTY-FIVE-YEAR FOLLOW-UP

Before professional college counseling services were known, Donald G. Paterson began, in the 1920s, a program of services at the University of Minnesota. Since that time, the program there has served as a model for numerous other institutions and as a training ground for many leaders in the field.

Minnesota is known also for its emphasis on empiricism in the sciences, an emphasis so strong and reminiscent of the hardships of drought and depression that coincided with the development of the experimental sciences in the U.S. that its approach is at times referred to as "dustbowl empiricism." This demand for evidence that procedures really work was felt in the evaluation of counseling services as soon as they were established. A significant early study by Williamson and Bordin (110) matched about 400 students who had come for counseling with 400 freshmen who had not come for counseling and compared their later school records. The counseled students made better scores on a scale of adjustment and better college grades.

Although one aim of counseling is to assist people with the solution of problems such as maintaining academic achievement or with adjustments to such events as an engagement or a new job, its ultimate aim is the improvement of the individual's pattern of handling life adjustments. Questions about the long-term effects of counseling were partially answered by a 25-year follow-up of the people included in the original Williamson-Bordin investigation.

After some persistent tracking, Campbell (17) was able to locate 99 percent of the original 384 matched pairs of subjects, and from the great majority of these, he was able to obtain usable data. Campbell's methods included a 30-page questionnaire devoted mainly to academic, personal, and vocational progress during college and afterward. Most of the subjects were also willing to grant a 30-minute interview, to retake the Strong Vocational Interest Blank, and to take the then current University of Minnesota entrance examination. Possible differences between the persons who had been counseled 25 years earlier and those who had not been counseled were examined.

Groups were matched, in the early Williamson-Bordin study, on the basis of scholastic aptitude; however, in later years, a number of students of varying aptitudes came in for counseling and needed to be shifted from the uncounseled group to the counseled group. In the later Campbell study, the late-counseled group were slightly different from the still uncounseled group. The counseled group scored slightly higher on measures of academic potential, and they seemed to be slightly higher on measures of anxiety or personal conflict. The counseled group included more first-born, who tend to have more adjustment problems, than did the uncounseled group.

Academic performance was, in an institution of higher education, a logical criterion for the evaluation of the effects of counseling. Although the counseled group was only slightly superior to the uncounseled in academic potential, the counseled group clearly performed more ably in college. Among the counseled students, the graduation rate at the bachelor's level was one quarter higher than among the uncounseled students. The difference was even more pronounced in advanced degrees. The counseled students tended to win more and higher academic honors; also, they participated more in activities and were elected to office more often than were the uncounseled students.

Not all of these differences can be attributed to counseling, and it would be unwarranted to say that counseling necessarily caused these things to happen to the students. Still, better performance in all aspects of college life, not just in courses or in graduation, was associated with counseling during the freshman year. By academic criteria, either counseling is a real asset to the individual, or individuals with non-intellectual assets (since intelligence was held constant) tend to make better use of the help of counselors. Counseling seems to have had some effect at the undergraduate level, and even more in graduate school.

Occupational measures showed that 25 years later, counseled students earned slightly higher annual salaries (about $1200 difference, which was not statistically significant) than did uncounseled students. According to a measure of contribution to society that included things such as professional honors, original plays, musical compositions, research, outstanding civic service, and assumption of executive responsibility, again the counseled students scored higher than did the uncounseled.

Personal adjustment reports also showed some differences between the counseled and the uncounseled students. Although the counseled students had in general done better in school and had more occupational achievements to their credit, they showed a tendency to feel less satisfaction with their achievements and to express greater concern about their adjustments, with some anxiety and some dissatisfaction with their lot in life. This finding was more evident among the counseled women, while the finding of greater occupational success was clearer among counseled men.

None of the differences between the counseled and the uncounseled students after 25 years were large, although some were clear. That there were any differences at all after such a period is interpreted as support for the case that counseling, as it was done at Minnesota in 1940, helped some men and women do somewhat better during the following quarter century than did those who did not seek help while in college.

As these former college students looked back on their counseling experience, most of them remembered it favorably, expressing the belief that it had been important in their educational program and progress during college. About 8 percent of the counseled students regarded counseling as the most important influence on their career decisions. It was in academic decision making that the students felt that counseling had been the most helpful.

Other evidence for the effectiveness of vocational counseling comes from England's National Institute of Industrial Psychology, which has conducted many studies of programs that helped young men to find suitable employment. Following samples of cases who had been counseled, investigators identified those who had followed plans made in consultation with the advisors and those who had not followed the general plans developed in the counseling sessions. When the levels of occupational satisfaction and of satisfactoriness to employers were compared, it was found that those who had followed the suggestions and counsel of the vocational counselors were better satisfied and more successful than were others. Vocational counseling was demonstrated to be associated with favorable occupational outcomes.

Vocational Counseling Today

Vocational counseling, or the process of helping individuals develop self-understanding and relate that understanding to occupations, is currently used in three major areas: the career decisions of youth, those of adults, and those of groups with special talents, handicaps, or characteristics.

TABLE 9–1. *Major applications of vocational counseling with three groups.*

Youth (Options)	Adults (Change)	Exceptional (Special Needs)
Higher education	Change based on technology	Gifted
Military service	Change based on age	Retarded
Labor market	Change based on interest	Physically handicapped
		Emotionally disturbed
		Women
		Religious and ethnic minorities

The Career Decisions of Youth

The idea of occupational choice-making that prevailed until the middle of this century was that a young man and his parents would look at the world of occupations, they would decide which looked possible and attractive, and the boy would enter the occupation. After the decision had been made, there was assumed to be no need later to reconsider or to change in most cases; the usual expectation, shown even in federal legislation on assistance to veterans, was that a person would follow the chosen career and would not need to change occupations. Interesting descriptions of this career-selection process are seen in early American literature, notably the autobiography of Benjamin Franklin, who described in some detail his own experience. Fortunately, in Franklin's case, his decision to become a printer did not prevent, but probably facilitated, his achievement in many other fields.

Today young people are still expected to make occupational choices and career plans, but not with the same finality as before. Instead of anticipating a lifetime in a job selected during youth, most people can look forward to having at least three occupations during their working years (careers), although there are still some occupations that people enter early and remain in late, such as medicine. For the majority of workers, a youthful decision is not the last, and maybe not even the most important, occupational choice.

SCHOOL GUIDANCE

The most obvious and widespread application of occupational psychology is in school guidance programs, although these sometimes emphasize other kinds of help for school children. Occupational information is included in the training of many school counselors. Occupational psychology has not been active enough, however, in organizing what is known about the psychological aspects of work and the processes of choosing an occupation. School counselors are armed primarily with measures of scholastic aptitudes, measures of vocational interests, and sometimes with occupational ability-pattern data based on the GATB. With the first types of information, the counselor can be of help in evaluating the chances of success in different school programs and of success and satisfaction in certain occupations. Personality-test data may help to identify students with handicapping personality problems or perhaps to suggest adjustments that might be of special difficulty, but they add little to the process of assisting in making career decisions.

The Career Options of Youth

Most youth who complete high school face a choice of three alternatives: higher education, the military, or the labor market.

HIGHER EDUCATION

More and more young people are choosing to continue their formal education beyond high school. With the opening of junior colleges and technical schools, in addition to the traditional colleges and universities, the opportunities for higher education are more plentiful. While this option was once limited to the privileged few, it is now viewed by many as a right, and it is becoming the modal choice of students graduating from high schools in the most affluent regions.

Higher education offers two primary orientations for a person's vocational development: these are exploration and preparation (93). *Exploration* gives the student the opportunity to keep his program broad and flexible. This exploration can be one of *continuing breadth*, as seen in schools that attempt to provide the classic liberal education. The emphasis is on the person and the general nature of knowledge, with little immediate concern for the relevance of the information to later employment. A second type of exploration is that of *finding focus: non-occupationally*. In this choice, the student may learn about different areas of knowledge, with the goal of determining those areas that are most important to him. This process does not necessarily include the application of the resulting self-knowledge to the choice of an occupation. Finally, a school may offer the chance for *finding focus: occupationally*. After taking a generalized curriculum, a student usually chooses a major, which leads to the choice of an occupation.

For those students who have made tentative decisions about their occupational futures when they enter college, higher education is more likely to be a setting that stresses *preparation* for the occupational world, either by crystallization or by specification. In *crystallization*, general vocational goals already decided upon are brought into sharper focus by exposure to material in the area of interest. For example, the decision to enter the field of medicine establishes some necessary requirements, but within the general requirements, there can still be some freedom in course work. *Specification*, on the other hand, is preparation for students who have made a fairly discrete vocational decision and are ready to begin training for an occupation. Some schools of engineering or architecture begin specialized courses as early as the first year. Such an education is explicit preparation for work and is most appropriate when basic issues of self-identity have been settled.

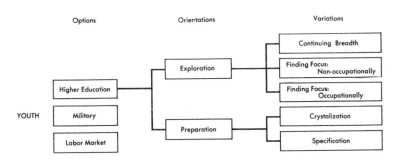

FIGURE 9-1. *Vocational orientations of higher education.*

MILITARY SERVICE

Students who do not choose to proceed to institutions of higher learning or technical training often drift into military service. This is sometimes a voluntary choice, but the world situation has, for a generation, required that most young men serve their country in one capacity or another. How the period of military service is handled varies with the individual and with conditions. Some succeed in using it as a worthwhile period, invested in the furthering of their career ambitions. On the other hand, the time in military service is frequently a period of marking time in a career, a time during which a person merely waits to return to civilian life.

THE LABOR MARKET

A substantial number of students finishing high school head directly for a job in business or industry. This was formerly the most common route. At present, however, the young person entering the labor market may find himself in a position not particularly favorable to beginning a career. Employers are reluctant to invest in training or breaking in a new man who has not yet met his military-service obligation. Besides the service problem, inexperienced and untried young people must compete with other more experienced applicants for positions at the same level. Despite these disadvantages, many young men and women enter the labor market immediately after high school, and in some cases even before, and begin occupational careers. That many of them, some 50 percent, flounder for several years is a reflection of the gap between school and work and of the vocational immaturity of the typical graduate.

Career Decisions of Adults

Vocational counseling is usually thought of as a service that schools provide for adolescent students, and the counseling of students is the major type of vocational counseling going on today. Observing the adult population, however, one can see the need for another kind of assistance in dealing with vocational problems. The vocational concerns of adults considering changes in their own occupational roles are numerous and real. Vocational changes are often forced on adults by technological changes, including invention and automation, or by similar external factors. Other developments that call for rethinking one's occupational activities include aging and the concomitant changes in capacities and interests.

CHANGES BASED ON TECHNOLOGY OR OTHER EXTERNAL FACTORS

Demands for skills, goods, and services are altered with progress, so that the number of workers in some jobs increases, while the workers on other jobs are phased out. The economy now demands workers in many specialties that did not even exist a few years ago. For example, the occupation of programmer did not exist twenty years ago, when computers were new and unfamiliar to the majority of Americans. Now almost every moderate-sized business uses a computer, and most people know what a computer is. Although it has put some men and women out of work, the computer has provided many opportunities for new and varied kinds of employment.

In addition to technological advances like the computer and automation, which have revolutionized some fields of work, other factors have had significant effects on the occupational structure and on men's careers. Public policy and legislation can create markets for certain products and, almost as quickly, eliminate markets. Some careers are terminated or altered by such factors as the depletion of natural resources, in which, for example, the ore fields or the mines no longer produce the raw material that provided work. Even in these times, when man increasingly seeks to control his environment, careers are still affected by natural events such as earthquakes or floods and by the misuse of resources as in water pollution, which can, in a moment or in a few years, eliminate a person's means of livelihood while creating a demand for other services.

CHANGES BASED ON AGE

In the United States, the number of citizens over the age of 65 has risen markedly in the past generation. The life plans of most workers in earlier generations called for beginning work shortly after becoming a teen-ager and continuing to work until death. Retirement was not a problem, because few workers actually retired. Now, however, what to do with the retirement years is an important consideration for many people. The question is not always whether or not to retire, because legal and corporate regulations in some cases insist that a person give up his job at 65 or 70. It is an interesting contradiction that, while there is a minimum age for public servants such as Congressmen and the President, there is no maximum age; thus, men are permitted to hold office long after their efficiency and effectiveness have waned considerably.

Retirement that is enjoyable and worthwhile requires planning. First, one must take into account the need for support: bills do not cease coming when employment ceases. Second, one must plan for an increased amount of free time: no job now dictates getting up and going to bed. It is possible to become quite discouraged with time on which no one makes demands and with activity that is not organized or purposeful. When these possible problems are foreseen, they can be minimized, and retirement can be a structured and meaningful part of a career.

It is not uncommon for an adult in his middle years to ask himself why he is doing what he does for a living. In serious reflection on this question, some workers find that the original reasons for their choices are no longer valid. The choice of an occupation in a spirit of youthful adventure, to please a parent who has since died, or to meet a pressing need that has since been alleviated are examples. As one experiences and learns, his attitudes change, and the thoughts and positions that led to his entering one kind of employment may not be relevant to his current thinking. When he has doubts, a person may turn to a professional counselor, instead of relying on the perspective, which may be limited or biased, of one who is personally involved or relying on someone who is at best an amateur. By applying the knowledge and using the tools of occupational psychology and of manpower economics, the counselor works with the adult in rethinking career goals in light of the current situation, resources, and perspectives.

Career Decisions of Exceptional Groups

In addition to the people who receive counseling in school guidance programs and the conventional adult counseling services, there is a large number of individuals who need special assistance. By virtue of inherited characteristics, accidents, and environment, these people constitute special groups. Included in these groups are the intellectually gifted, the retarded, the physically handicapped, the emotionally disturbed, women, and various ethnic and religious groups such as blacks in the U.S. and non-blacks in some African countries, and Jews in Soviet Russia and non-Jews in Israel.

The intellectually gifted receive special attention because they have exceptional promise. In times when creative solutions to civilization's problems are needed, society must make the best use of talent. The public school system, with its responsibility for educating unprecedented numbers of children, finds it difficult to tailor the educational process to fit each student. Those with special and outstanding talents need special educational opportunities to maximize development of their potential. Thus, vocational counseling for the gifted requires an approach somewhat different from that appropriate for others.

THE RETARDED

Also exceptional, in the sense that they too differ in intelligence from the majority of children, are the mentally retarded. Like the gifted, the retarded do not fit well into the usual pattern and process of public education. For years the retarded were ignored or merely segregated, but as new emphasis has been placed on human values and a degree of affluence has been attained to support it, attention and money have been directed to understanding the causes and cures of retardation. As better understanding is attained, new programs and strategies are being developed for these handicapped individuals. As general knowledge of employment demands and job requirements increases, the retarded can fill a special need for workers who will be satisfied with repetitive activity that provides little variety and little challenge. There are some jobs in which employers find that the mentally retarded are more successful than workers who are not retarded. Improved vocational counseling by professional counselors of the retarded can help to produce better satisfied and more productive retardates, as well as contribute to a more efficient economy.

THE PHYSICALLY HANDICAPPED

In recent years, great strides have been made in the rehabilitation of physically handicapped persons. Vocational rehabilitation, the process of assisting handicapped people in their work adjustment, has been the focus of interesting work in vocational development. At the University of Minnesota, staff members of the Industrial Relations Center are developing a theory of work adjustment designed to be applicable not only to those who make vocational adjustments despite handicaps and with the help of rehabilitation, but also to all who are engaged in vocational training or who are employed. Recognizing work as one important link to reality, many psychologists have stressed the importance of a man's work in his life. In the rehabilitation of a handicapped person, vocational rehabilitation serves as a major focus for the process of restoring people to active participation in society.

As with any group, vocational counseling with the physically handicapped is directed toward the development of a realistic self-concept and toward relating that self-concept to the occupational world. With the handicapped, perhaps more than with other groups, the counselor must attempt to deal with the attitudes of the individual. Individuals who have been handicapped since before their working days may have adapted well to their difficulty, but they may have developed a manner that is more completely dependent than necessary. For those who incur a disability during their working years, the first step in the rehabilitation process is to learn to live with the handicap. In these cases, knowledge about career patterns and life stages can be helpful to the individual attempting to regain a realistic perspective on his own career.

THE EMOTIONALLY DISTURBED

The emotionally disturbed are another group requiring special assistance in vocational counseling. Their needs and attitudes prevent them from making the usual adjustments to life's demands. In their lives, the job situation can be of more than customary importance; therefore, it takes on special meaning, and special care in choice is necessary. Occupational therapy, consisting of work-type activities selected for their therapeutic value, is sometimes used for exploration or for training in effective work habits in the counseling and rehabilitation of the emotionally disturbed. With this special group, vocational counseling relies heavily on personality theory and psychotherapy as well as on occupational psychology.

Positive results from vocational counseling with the emotionally disturbed are illustrated in a Veterans Administration study (106), which gathered employment information from a random sample of 1421 emotionally disturbed veterans of World War II and the Korean Conflict. At the time of the study, seven of every ten nonhospitalized veterans were employed. The distribution of these veterans in the labor force was similar to that of the general population, indicating that these men were not limited to a few occupations. Ninety percent of the employed veterans were making a satisfactory adjustment, and the overall record of the men showed that, contrary to many stereotypes, rate of turnover was not a problem for these men with a history of emotional disturbance. Findings such as these are encouraging and show how well some emotionally disturbed individuals who receive vocational counseling can adjust to work.

WOMEN

Few would quarrel with the position that women are a special group and, as such, need special consideration. Early in this century, the problem of women in the labor market was not an issue because, in their subservient role, middle-class women stayed at home and did what was expected of them. With the modern recognition of women as persons and as possessors of talents that they can bring to the economy, the role of the woman in the labor force is becoming more important. The special role that they play in the family means, however, that their careers have some distinctive characteristics and that they need special help in vocational counseling. The career patterns of men are fairly well understood, but only now are we beginning to study and to understand the career patterns of women. The problems of reconciling family and career demands lie at the heart of the counseling of women.

In order for women to have equal opportunities and rewards for their work, ultimately the societal attitudes toward women and their working must change. In the meantime, some progress can be made through vocational counseling for women. Such counseling can help by broadening women's horizons and expectations, otherwise limited by cultural mores and traditions. As noted in a recent report of the Presidential Commission on the Status of American Women, education and counseling must be made more relevant to their needs so that, from an earlier age, women develop less stereotyped and more personally realistic ideas about their possible roles in the occupational world.

RELIGIOUS AND ETHNIC MINORITIES

It is not difficult to see the effects of membership in religious and ethnic minorities on career development. Although some minorities have overcome the extra problems experienced by their groups, and some minority groups have even excelled in certain occupations—for example, the Irish in politics, Jews in commerce, and Negroes in athletics—very often a minority group member suffers discrimination in occupational activities as well as in other areas of life. The effects on careers and occupations begin early in a person's life, since cultural expectations are taught from an early age. By the time a person reaches high school, if indeed he gets that far, his aspirations and his preparation can already have limiting effects on his career plans and achievements.

Recently there have been more informed recognition and attempts to change discriminatory practices and effects. Major changes here require major social action, in which vocational counseling can play a role. Expanded opportunities must be developed, in conjunction with realistic and maximum goals, for members of minorities. When accompanied by the best possible planning and preparation on the part of minority group members, vocational counseling can be instrumental in their more successful occupational adjustment.

Trends in Vocational Counseling

Vocational counseling is the process of assisting individuals in making vocational decisions and adjustments in their quest for personal development and for self-realization in society. Its formal beginnings involved the model of measuring the man, measuring the job, and matching the man and the job. Vocational counseling was then broadened to include more than the choosing of an occupation: the search for personal identity is now paramount in vocational counseling. A man's occupational life is seen as one part, but a central part, of his existence.

From early in this century, through two world wars, and in our present rapidly evolving economy, vocational counseling has become an important factor in the social scene. It is now an integral part of the educational system, the employment system, and the services to exceptional persons whether gifted or handicapped. What is in store for the future of vocational guidance and counseling?

Technological advances have their impact on vocational counseling as on other areas of educational life. These advances have led to improved tools in the form of tests and job descriptions and improved methods in the form of interview procedures, and hence to more effectiveness in work with individuals and groups.

The major technological advance of recent years, which may ultimately have a revolutionizing impact on counseling, is the electronic computer and its terminals for the storage and retrieval of information. The use of computers in counseling is not only recent but still experimental. Several projects are now actively working on the problems of making computers useful in counseling (12), among them the *Information System for Vocational Decisions,* directed by David Tiedeman, Allen Ellis, and Robert O'Hara at Harvard University, and the *Educational and Career Exploration System,* being developed by Frank Minor of the International Business Machines Corporation with the cooperation of consultants (Donald Super and Roger Myers) at Teachers College, Columbia University.

Both of these systems are designed to have the computer perform the functions that can best be performed by a machine and thus to help the counselor with those activities in which a real human being can be most effective in helping another human being. The properly programmed machine can, for example, provide rapid, accurate, and dynamic information about educational opportunities, occupations, and job openings. The machine can help the individual compare his own strengths and weaknesses with the demands of colleges and of jobs, although the counselor can respond more adequately to the feelings that this comparison may arouse. The informed client and the human counselor can discuss the client's reactions as he works through his decisions, his commitment to act on them, and his possible plans.

The role of the counselor has been defined as that of facilitator of individual development. It has more recently been pointed out that to be most effective, the counselor must learn to work not only with individuals and groups, but also with the societal structures that, to a large extent, determine the conditions in which people develop. The counselor is not necessarily limited to a one-to-one relationship in effecting changes in life styles. Besides making the most of his own personal characteristics in counseling, the counselor should use whatever external means are appropriate and effective.

Summary

This chapter has dealt with the applications of occupational psychology in vocational guidance and counseling. The origins of the vocational guidance movement as an effort to help out-of-school youth, as well as the mental testing, mental health, and psychotherapeutic developments which shaped it, were discussed.

Research shows that people who have had professional vocational counseling believe that they have profited from the experience. Over long time spans, those who have been counseled are demonstrably more successful and happier than are matched individuals who have not been counseled. Today vocational counseling is concerned not only with the adolescents in school and college, but also with adults at work, in search of work, and retiring from work, and with individuals in special circumstances or with special handicaps. Vocational counseling has become more effective as it increases its use of the findings, methods, and instruments of occupational psychology and of related technologies.

references

1. Allport, G. W., and Vernon, P. E. *Study of values: A scale for measuring the dominant interests in personality.* Boston: Houghton Mifflin, 1931.
2. Allport, G. W., Vernon, P. E., and Lindzey, G. *Study of values: A scale for measuring dominant interests in personality.* Boston: Houghton Mifflin, 1960. 3rd Ed.
3. American Psychological Association. *Ethical standards of psychologists.* Washington, 1953.
4. American Psychological Association. Testing and public policy. *Amer. Psychologist*, 1965, 20, 857–992.
5. American Psychological Association. *Standards for educational and psychological tests and manuals.* Washington, 1966.
6. Anastasi, A. *Psychological testing.* New York: Macmillan, 1968, 3rd Ed.
7. Bell, H. M. *Matching youth and jobs.* Washington: American Council on Education, 1940.
8. Bemis, S. E. Occupational validity of the General Aptitude Test Battery. *J. appl. Psychol.*, 1968, 52, 240–244.
9. Berdie, R. F. Prediction of college achievement and satisfaction. *J. appl. Psychol.*, 1944, 28, 239–245.
10. Bingham, W. C. Change of occupation as a function of the regnancy of occupational self concepts. Unpubl. doctoral dissertation; New York: Teachers College, Columbia University, 1966.
11. Bohn, M. J., Jr., and Super, D. E. The computer in counseling and guidance programs. *Educ. Technol.*, 1969, 9, 29–31.
12. Blocher, D. H., and Schutz, R. A. Relationships among self-descriptions, occupational stereotypes, and vocational preferences. *J. couns. Psychol.*, 1961, 8, 314–317.
13. Bordin, E. S. A theory of vocational interests as dynamic phenomena. *Educ. psychol. Measmt.*, 1943, 3, 49–66.
14. Bordin, E. S., Nachmann, B., and Segal, S. J. An articulated framework for vocational development. *J. couns. Psychol.*, 1963, 10, 107–117.
15. Borow, H. (Ed.). *Man in a world at work.* Boston: Houghton Mifflin, 1964.
16. Brophy, A. L. Self, role, and satisfaction. *Genetic Psychol. Monographs*, 1959, 59, 263–308.

17. Campbell, D. P. *The results of counseling: Twenty-five years later.* Philadelphia: Saunders, 1965.

18. Campbell, D. P. *Manual for Strong Vocational Interest Blanks.* Stanford, Calif.: Stanford Univ. Press, 1966.

19. Carter, H. D. The development of vocational attitudes. *J. consult. Psychol.,* 1940, *4,* 185–191.

20. Centers, R. Motivational aspects of occupational stratification. *J. soc. Psychol.,* 1948, *28,* 187–217.

21. Clark, K. E. *The vocational interests of nonprofessional men.* Minneapolis: Univ. Minn. Press, 1961.

22. Crites, J. O. *Vocational psychology.* New York: McGraw-Hill, 1969.

23. Cronbach, L. J. *Essentials of psychological testing.* New York: Harper & Row, 1960. 2nd Ed.

24. *Dictionary of Occupational Titles.* Washington: U.S. Department of Labor, 1965. 3rd Ed.

25. Dunnette, M. D. *Personnel selection and placement.* Belmont, Calif.: Wadsworth, 1966.

26. Dvorak, B. J. The General Aptitude Test Battery. *Pers. guid. J.,* 1956, *35,* 145–154.

27. Earle, F. M. *Psychology and the choice of a career.* London: Methuen, 1933.

28. Edwards, A. L. *The social desirability variable in personality assessment and research.* New York: Holt, Rinehart and Winston, 1957.

29. Ewen, R. B. Some determinants of job satisfaction: A study of the generality of Herzberg's theory. *J. appl. Psychol.,* 1964, *48,* 161–163.

30. Flanagan, J. C. *The Aviation Psychology Program in the AAF.* ("AAF Aviation Psychology Report," No. 1), Washington: Government Printing Office, 1948.

31. Flanagan, J. C. The critical incident technique. *Psychol. Bull.,* 1954, *51,* 327–358.

32. Flanagan, J. C., *et al. Design for a study of American youth.* Boston: Houghton Mifflin, 1962.

33. Flanagan, J. C., *et al. The American high school student.* Pittsburgh: Univ. Pittsburgh Press, 1964.

34. Flanagan, J. C., and Cooley, W. W. *Project Talent: One year follow-up studies.* Pittsburgh: Univ. Pittsburgh Press, 1966.

35. Friedman, F. A., and Havighurst, R. J. *The meaning of work and retirement.* Chicago: Univ. Chicago Press, 1954.

36. Fryer, D. Occupational intelligence standards. *School and Society,* 1922, *16,* 273–277.

37. *General Aptitude Test Battery, Section II: Scoring directions and norms; Section III: Development.* Washington: U.S. Department of Labor, 1958, 1962.

38. Getzels, J. W., and Guba, E. G. Role, role conflict, and effectiveness. *Amer. Sociol. Rev.,* 1954, *19,* 164–174.

39. Ghiselli, E. E. *The validity of occupational aptitude tests.* New York: Wiley, 1966.

40. Ginzberg, E., Ginsburg, S. W., Axelrad, S., and Herma, J. L. *Occupational choice.* New York: Columbia Univ. Press, 1951.

41. Goldman, L. *Using tests in counseling.* New York: Appleton-Century-Crofts, 1961.

42. Goslin, D. A. *The search for ability.* New York: Russell Sage, 1963.

43. Gribbons, W. D., and Lohnes, P. R. *Emerging careers.* New York: Teachers College Press, 1968.

44. Guilford, J. P., Christensen, P. R., Bond, N. A., Jr., and Sutton, M. A. A factor analysis of human interests. *Psychol. Monographs,* 1954, No. 375.

45. Hall, C. S., and Lindzey, G. *Theories of personality.* New York: Wiley, 1957.

46. Harris, D. Group differences in values within a university. *J. abnorm. social Psychol.,* 1934, *29,* 95–102.

47. Havighurst, R. J. *Human development and education.* New York: David McKay Co., 1953.

48. Herzberg, F., Mausner, B., Peterson, R. O., and Capwell, D. F. *Job attitudes: Review of research and opinion.* Pittsburgh: Psychological Service of Pittsburgh, 1957.

49. Holland, J. L. A theory of vocational choice. *J. Couns. Psychol.,* 1959, *6,* 35–44.

50. Hoppock, R. *Job satisfaction.* New York: Harper, 1935.

51. Hulin, C. L. Job satisfaction and turnover in a female clerical population. *J. appl. Psychol.,* 1966, *50,* 280–285.

52. Hulin, C. L. Effects of changes in job-satisfaction levels on employee turnover. *J. appl. Psychol.,* 1968, *52,* 122–126.

53. James, W. *Principles of psychology.* New York: Holt, 1890.

54. Kates, S. L. Rorschach responses related to vocational interests and job satisfaction. *Psychol. Monographs,* 1950, No. 309.

55. Kates, S. L. Rorschach responses, Strong Blank scores and job satisfaction among policemen. *J. appl. Psychol.,* 1950, *34,* 249–354.

56. Kelly, G. A. *Psychology of personal constructs.* New York: Norton, 1955.

57. Kinnane, J. F., and Gaubinger, J. R. Life values and work values. *J. Couns. Psychol.,* 1963, *10,* 363–367.

58. Kirkpatrick, J. J., Ewen, R. B., Barrett, R. S., and Katzell, R. A. *Testing and fair employment.* New York: New York Univ. Press, 1968.

59. Lawshe, C. H., and Balma, M. J. *Principles of personnel testing.* New York: McGraw-Hill, 1966. 2nd Ed.

60. LoCascio, R. Delayed and impaired vocational development: A neglected aspect of vocational development theory. *Pers. guid. J.,* 1964, *42,* 885–887.

61. Lohnes, P. R. Markov models for human development research. *J. Couns. Psychol.,* 1965, *12,* 322–327.

62. Maslow, A. H. *Motivation and personality.* New York: Harper, 1954.

63. Mead, G. H. *Mind, self, and society.* Chicago: Univ. Chicago Press, 1934.

64. Miller, D. C., and Form, W. H. *Industrial sociology.* New York: Harper, 1951.

65. Morrison, R. L., Self-concept implementation in occupational choices. *J. Couns. Psychol.,* 1962, *9,* 255–260.

66. Murray, H. A. (Ed.). *Explorations in personality.* New York: Oxford Univ. Press, 1938.

67. Nachmann, B. Childhood experience and vocational choice in law, dentistry, and social work. *J. Couns. Psychol.,* 1960, *7,* 243–250.

68. National Vocational Guidance Association. Principles and practices of vocational guidance. *Occupations,* 1937, *15,* 772–778.

69. Normile, R. H. Differentiating among known occupational groups by means of the Work Values Inventory. Unpub. doctoral dissertation; Washington: Catholic Univ. of America, 1967.

70. Oppenheimer, E. A. The relationship between certain self construct and occupational preferences. *J. Couns. Psychol.,* 1966, *13,* 191–197.

71. Parsons, F. *Choosing a vocation.* Boston: Houghton Mifflin, 1909.

72. Paterson, D. G., *et al. The Minnesota Mechanical Abilities Tests.* Minneapolis: Univ. Minn. Press, 1930.

73. Paterson, D. G., and Darley, J. G. *Men, women, and jobs.* Minneapolis: Univ. Minn. Press, 1936.

74. Roe, A. *The psychology of occupations.* New York: Wiley, 1956.

75. Roe, A., and Siegelman, M. *The origin of interests.* Washington: American Personnel and Guidance Association, 1964.

76. Rosenberg, M. *Occupations and values.* New York: Free Press, 1957.

77. Rothney, J. W. M. *Guidance practices and results.* New York: Harper & Row, 1958.

78. Schaefer, B. R. The validity and utility of the Allport-Vernon Study of Values test. *J. abnorm. social Psychol.*, 1936, 30, 419–422.
79. Schaffer, R. H. Job satisfaction as related to need satisfaction in work. *Psychol. Monographs*, 1953, No. 364.
80. Schwebel, M. *The interests of pharmacists.* New York: Columbia Univ. Press, 1951.
81. Shartle, C. L. *Occupational information.* Englewood Cliffs, N. J.: Prentice-Hall, 1959.
82. Simpson, R. L., and Simpson, I. H. Values, personal influence, and occupational choice. *Social Forces*, 1960, 39, 116–125.
83. Stead, W. H., and Shartle, C. L. *Occupational counseling techniques.* New York: American Book Co., 1940.
84. Stephenson, R. R. Occupational choice as a crystallized self-concept. *J. couns. Psychol.*, 1961, 8, 211–216.
85. Stewart, N. AGCT scores of Army personnel grouped by occupation. *Occupations*, 1947, 26, 5–41.
86. Stone, C. H., and Kendall, W. E. *Effective personnel selection procedures.* Englewood Cliffs, N. J.: Prentice-Hall, 1956.
87. Stone, C. L. The personality factor in vocational guidance. *J. abnorm. social Psychol.*, 1933, 28, 274–275.
88. Strong, E. K., Jr. *Vocational interests of men and women.* Stanford, Calif.: Stanford Univ. Press, 1943.
89. Strong, E. K., Jr. *Vocational interests 18 years after college.* Minneapolis: Univ. Minn. Press, 1955.
90. Super, D. E. The criteria of vocational success. *Occupations*, 1951, 29, 5–8.
91. Super, D. E. Career patterns as a basis for vocational counseling. *J. couns. Psychol.*, 1954, 1, 12–20.
92. Super, D. E. *The psychology of careers.* New York: Harper, 1957.
93. Super, D. E. Goal specificity in the vocational counseling of future college students. *Pers. guid. J.*, 1964, 43, 127–134.
94. Super, D. E. *The Work Values Inventory.* Boston: Houghton Mifflin, 1969.
95. Super, D. E., and Crites, J. O. *Appraising vocational fitness.* New York: Harper & Row, 1962. Rev. Ed.
96. Super, D. E., Crites, J. O., Hummel, R. C., Moser, H. P., Overstreet, P. L., and Warnath, C. *Vocational development: A framework for research.* New York: Teachers College Press, 1957.
97. Super, D. E., Kowalski, R. S., and Gotkin, E. H. Floundering and trial after high school. Cooperative Research Project No. 1393. New York: Teachers College, Columbia University, 1967.

98. Super, D. E., Starishevsky, R., Matlin, N., and Jordaan, J. P. *Career development: Self-concept theory.* New York: College Entrance Examination Board, 1963.
99. Thompson, A. S., and Super, D. E. (Eds.). *The professional preparation of counseling psychologists.* New York: Teachers College Bureau of Publications, 1964.
100. Thorndike, R. L. *Personnel selection.* New York: Wiley, 1949.
101. Thorndike, R. L., and Hagen, E. *Ten thousand careers.* New York: Wiley, 1959.
102. Thumin, F. Personality characteristics of diverse occupational groups. *Pers. guid. J.,* 1965, *45,* 468–470.
103. Tiedeman, D. V. Decision and vocational development: A paradigm and its implications. *Pers. guid. J.,* 1961, *40,* 15–20.
104. Tiedeman, D. V., O'Hara, R. P., and Matthews, E. Position choices and careers: Elements of a theory. *Harvard Studies in Career Development,* No. 8. Cambridge, Mass.: Harvard Grad. Sch. of Education, 1958.
105. Tutton, M. E. Stability of adolescent vocational interest. *Vocational Guidance Quarterly,* 1955, *3,* 78–80.
106. Veterans Administration, Department of Veterans Benefits. *They return to work.* Washington: Government Printing Office, 1963.
107. Vroom, V. H. *Some personality determinants of the effects of participation.* Englewood Cliffs, N. J.: Prentice-Hall, 1960.
108. Vroom, V. H. *Work and motivation.* New York: Wiley, 1964.
109. Walsh, R. P. The effects of needs on responses to job duties. *J. couns. Psychol.,* 1959, *6,* 194–198.
110. Williamson, E. G., and Bordin, E. S. Evaluating counseling by means of a control-group experiment. *School and Society,* 1940, *52,* 434–440.
111. Wispé, L. G. A sociometric analysis of conflicting role-expectancies. *Amer. J. Sociol.,* 1955, *61,* 134–137.
112. Wylie, R. *The self concept.* Lincoln: Univ. Nebraska Press, 1961.
113. Yerkes, R. M. (Ed.). Psychological examining in the U.S. Army. *Memoirs of the National Academy of Sciences,* 1921, *15,* 819–837.

readings

As an introduction to occupational psychology, this volume provides brief coverage of current issues and trends in the field. The topics of these chapters have been discussed in more detail by other texts and treatises. For readers interested in pursuing a specific topic further, some suggested books are listed here in conjunction with the chapters to which they are most relevant.

CHAPTER 2 How People Differ

Anastasi, A. *Differential psychology*. New York: Macmillan, 1963.
Bloom, B. *Stability and change in human characteristics*. New York: Wiley, 1964.
Hunt, J. McV. *Intelligence and experience*. New York: Ronald Press, 1961.
Tyler, L. E. *The psychology of human differences*. New York: Appleton-Century-Crofts, 1965.

CHAPTER 3 Some Problems of Assessment and Measurement

Cronbach, L. J. *Essentials of psychological testing*. New York: Harper & Row, 1969. 3rd Ed.
Dunnette, M. D. *Personnel selection and placement*. Belmont, Calif.: Wadsworth, 1966.
Goslin, D. A. *The search for ability*. New York: Russell Sage, 1963.
Super, D. E., and Crites, J. O. *Appraising vocational fitness*. New York: Harper & Row, 1962. Rev. Ed.
Thorndike, R. L., and Hagen, E. *Measurement and evaluation in psychology and education*. New York: Wiley, 1969. 3rd Ed.
Tyler, L. E. *Tests and measurements*. Englewood Cliffs, N.J.: Prentice-Hall, 1963.

CHAPTER 4 Occupational Ability and Aptitude Patterns

Crites, J. O. *Vocational psychology*. New York: McGraw-Hill, 1969.
General Aptitude Test Battery, Section III: Development. Washington: U.S. Department of Labor, 1962.

Herzberg, F., Mausner, B., and Snyderman, B. B. *The motivation to work.* New York: Wiley, 1959.

Roe, A. *Psychology of occupations.* New York: Wiley, 1956.

Thorndike, R. L., and Hagen, E. *Ten thousand careers.* New York: Wiley, 1959.

Vroom, V. H. *Work and motivation.* New York: Wiley, 1964.

CHAPTER 5   Occupational Personality Patterns

Crites, J. O. *Vocational psychology.* New York: McGraw-Hill, 1969.

Holland, J. L. *The psychology of vocational choice.* Waltham, Mass.: Blaisdell, 1966.

Osipow, S. H. *Theories of career development.* New York: Appleton-Century-Crofts, 1968.

Roe, A. *The psychology of occupations.* New York: Wiley, 1956.

Rosenberg, M. *Occupations and values.* New York: Free Press, 1957.

Strong, E. K., Jr. *Vocational interests 18 years after college.* Minneapolis: Univ. Minn. Press, 1955.

Super, D. E., Starishevsky, R., Matlin, N., and Jordaan, J. P. *Career development: Self-concept theory.* New York: College Entrance Examination Board, 1963.

CHAPTER 6   Occupations versus Careers

Osipow, S. H. *Theories of career development.* New York: Appleton-Century-Crofts, 1968.

Super, D. E. *The psychology of careers.* New York: Harper & Row, 1957.

Zytowski, D. (Ed.). *Vocational behavior: Readings in theory and research.* New York: Holt, Rinehart and Winston, 1968.

CHAPTER 7   How Careers Unfold

Crites, J. O. *Vocational psychology.* New York: McGraw-Hill, 1969.

Kroll, A. M., *et al. Career development: Growth and crisis.* New York: Wiley, 1970.

Miller, D. C., and Form, W. H. *Industrial sociology.* New York: Harper & Row, 1964. Rev. Ed.

Super, D. E. *The psychology of careers.* New York: Harper & Row, 1957.

Super, D. E., Starishevsky, R., Matlin, N., and Jordaan, J. P. *Career development: Self-concept theory.* New York: College Entrance Examination Board, 1963.

Tiedeman, D. V., and O'Hara, R. P. *Career development: Choice and adjustment.* New York: College Entrance Examination Board, 1963.

CHAPTER 8   Personnel Selection and Development

Dunnette, M. D. *Personnel selection and placement.* Belmont, Calif.: Wadsworth, 1966.

Maynard, H. B. (Ed.). *The management handbook.* New York: McGraw-Hill, 1960.

Super, D. E., and Crites, J. O. *Appraising vocational fitness.* New York: Harper & Row, 1962. Rev. Ed.

CHAPTER 9   Vocational Guidance and Counseling

Bordin, E. S. *Psychological counseling.* New York: Appleton-Century-Crofts, 1968. 2nd Ed.

Borow, H. (Ed.). *Man in a world at work.* Boston: Houghton Mifflin, 1964.

Hansen, L. S. *Career development practices in school and community.* Washington: National Vocational Guidance Association, 1970.

Tyler, L. E. *The work of the counselor.* New York: Appleton-Century-Crofts, 1969. 3rd Ed.

Viteles, M. S., Brayfield, A. H., and Tyler, L. E. *Vocational counseling: A reappraisal in honor of Donald G. Paterson.* Minnesota Studies in Student Personnel Work, No. 11. Minneapolis: Univ. Minn. Press, 1961.

index